What It Takes To Be a Teacher

The Role of Personal and Professional Development

Penny A. Freppon

with

Andrew Allen

JoAnn Archie

Karen Morrow Durica

Jack George

John Greenwell

Kris Gregory

Ruth Heil

Donna Ware

Phyllis Whitin

HEINEMANN
Portsmouth, NH

This book is dedicated to the contributing teachers Andrew Allen, JoAnn Archie, Karen Morrow Durica, Jack George, John Greenwell, Kris Gregory, Ruth Heil, Donna Ware, and Phyllis Whitin. My deepest appreciation and profound respect for who you are and all that you do for children. (And just think, dear friends, we did this book in cyberspace!)

Heinemann
A division of Reed Elsevier Inc.
361 Hanover Street
Portsmouth, NH 03801–3912
www.heinemann.com

Offices and agents throughout the world

The author and publisher wish to thank those who have generously given permission to reprint borrowed material:

"Octopus" by Ogden Nash, Copyright © 1942 by Ogden Nash, renewed. Reprinted by permission of Curtis Brown, Ltd., New York, and Carlton Books, London.

"Teaching Tools" by Michelle McAfee is reprinted from *Teaching Tolerance Magazine,* Spring 2001. Copyright © 2001 by Teaching Tolerance, Southern Poverty Law Center, Montgomery, Alabama. Reprinted by permission.

Excerpts from "'I Don't Want to Read This': Students Responses to Illustrations of Black Characters in Children's Picture Books" by Andrew M. A. Allen in *Educating African Canadians* edited by Karen S. Brathwaite and Carle E. James. Copyright © 1996 by Our Schools/Our Selves Educational Foundation. Published by James Lorimer and Company, Ltd. Reprinted by permission of Our Schools/Our Selves Educational Foundation.

Adaptation of "Differences Between Strategies and Skills" is from the *American Federation of Teachers' Educational Research and Dissemination (ER&D) Reading Comprehension Instruction Manual.* Copyright © 2000 by the American Federation of Teachers. Reprinted with permission.

Library of Congress Cataloging-in-Publication Data
What it takes to be a teacher : the role of personal and professional development /
Penny A. Freppon [et al.].
 p. cm.
 Includes bibliographical references and index.
 ISBN 0-325-00371-8
 1. Teachers—Psychology. 2. Teachers—In-service training. 3. Teaching. I. Freppon, Penny A.

LB1775 .W428 2001
371.1'0023—dc21
 2001024853

Editor: Danny Miller
Production service: Lisa Garboski, bookworks
Production coordinator: Elizabeth Valway
Cover design: Joni Doherty Design
Manufacturing: Steve Bernier

Printed in the United States of America on acid-free paper
05 04 03 02 01 DA 1 2 3 4 5

Contents

Foreword

You may know, or you will soon discover, that teaching is always in motion and never standing still, that it is an act of invention and becoming, an enterprise characterized by discovery and surprise. You may know that teaching is dynamic; necessary preparation, planning, and organization is in the service of a stunning paradox: teaching is improvisational and idiosyncratic, its best moments are neither entirely anticipated nor easily predicted.

Teachers can bring to their efforts knowledge, compassion, awareness, and engagement; they might bring as well a set of explicit commitments, articulated values, and dreams and goals. These might then, if thought through enough, if well-enough developed, help teachers chart their various courses and navigate their diverse journeys. But there is no definitive map to draw upon, no completed blueprint to consult, for the journey of teaching is a trip into the human heart, the living mind, as infinite, inexact, excruciating, and dazzling as, say, falling in love.

Teaching, like love, is necessarily imperfect, constitutively unfinished. It is, as the teachers in this book demonstrate, a journey. The best teaching is always in search of better teaching. In fact, what makes good teaching distinctive is the unremitting force of the quest. It is in the search that we resist being turned into clerks or functionaries or objects.

Teaching is an energetic vocation—the people who do it well bring intellectual and moral energy to bear in every dimension. Teachers need to fight to stay wide awake, that is, to see their students as three-dimensional and unique in institutions gone mad on normalizing labels and ironclad categories, and to see the world as it really is against all the anesthetizing, conformist pressures and flatting effects of modern society. Teachers need to fight to fully embrace their students' lives even as they nourish and challenge each one to stand up and seize an education that will make a difference. This book, *What It Takes to be a Teacher*, provides wonderful examples of just this kind of teaching.

"If I only had a home . . . a heart . . . a brain . . . the nerves." Teachers who want to make a difference might borrow from the four hopeful seekers skipping down the yellow brick road toward Oz. Each has diagnosed a deficiency, identified a lack, and recognized a need. Each is conscious of something missing, a hole in need of repair. Each is stirred to action against an obstacle to his or her fullness, and each gathers power and momentum from others, from intimate relationships forged through collective struggles.

Of course, we can now know in advance that there is no way out at the end of the road, no higher power with a magic wand to solve our problems. We look, then, inside ourselves, summon the strengths we didn't know we had, connect up with parents and students, fellow teachers and citizens to create the schools and classrooms we all deserve—thoughtful places of decency, sites of peace and justice. We are on the way, then, to the real Emerald Cities.

William Ayers
Distinguished Professor
at the University of Illinois at Chicago.
Author of *Fugitive Days* (Beacon Press).

Preface

I am most fortunate to spend some of the summer in a place about 15 miles from Yellowstone National Park. There, I am a member of a women's hiking group that returns year after year to spend as much time as possible in this stunningly beautiful place.

Our group began in the 1980s with three women who began to meet to hike together with their dogs. They were known at that time as the "Ladies and the Bitches." Gradually, and then rapidly, their numbers grew, and the dogs were left at home. Dogs attract grizzly bears, who also enjoy the wonderful environs.

Now, we number from thirty to fifty per hike and call ourselves "The WOWs" or "women of the wild" (not to be confused with wild old women). We are females of all ages who hike and often include our daughters and granddaughters. Sometimes sons and grandsons are included as guests. We've had a little boy with us since he was seven months old. He has traveled on his mother's back or in the arms of a grandmother walking beside her.

We are of diverse social and economic groups from all over the United States and abroad. In spite of our many fundamental differences, we have a united goal of learning more about the place we so enjoy. Of course, another goal is companionship and the pleasure of being a member of this community. On our hikes, we are able to explore new territory with strong, interesting people, getting to know the lay of the land and seeing splendid vistas. We share the experience of exhaustion and a deep sense of accomplishment that makes work or play of any kind truly valuable. Importantly, we have a feeling of knowing and belonging.

During our hikes together, we listen to and participate in conversations about how each of us came to be in this place. Of interest are stories of what attracted us initially and what sustains us as we find the time and energy it takes to stay in this place as long as possible. Each story tells of satisfaction and of sacrifice. We're glad to have accomplished the journeys that led us to new knowledge and achievement in the mountains. Our paths have not been without their challenges; yet we are compelled to make the trip. And so we return year after year, meeting the challenge of the trail and learning how to make a life and find a way of being in this place.

Becoming a good teacher involves just this kind of sustained search, adaptation, sacrifice, and true satisfaction. On the journey toward effective teaching, we travel to a significant place and experience splendid vistas, struggles, and achievements. Learning to teach and becoming happy in teaching sends us on a trek toward a sense of belonging. Belonging provides an authentic way of *being* in the profession. As on a mountain journey, a teacher's work is accomplished on one's own and with the support of others. Special aspects of teaching—such as caring and intellectual curiosity—are some of the things that compel teachers to search for meaning in their own lives. Teachers engage in taking risks, as they understand more about the journey of learning to teach. This is the substance that sustains the construction of an effective teaching practice.

Penny Freppon

Acknowledgments

As in the writing of any book there are many people without whom the book would not be written. Thus, I thank especially Ellen McIntyre for her hard work and many contributions. I am extremely grateful to Regie Routman for her recognition that the manuscript had something to offer and to Lois Bridges for providing invaluable and generous support. Thank you, Gerald Coles, your suggestions helped a great deal. Danny Miller, your editing expertise and good humor have made all the difference. I'll always be grateful.

My most sincere thanks to Jane West at Agnes Scott College and her students, Beth Godbee, Betty Callahan, Selyka Givan, Abby Dougherty, and Currey Hitchens, who read and commented on the manuscript. To Colleen Bonnes, Cathy Rosemary, and Kathy Rosko, my affection and gratitude for your phone calls, e-mails, and scholarly input. Thanks to Katrina Bowling for excellent reference work. To colleagues at NRC, NCTE, IRA, and AERA, every word of encouragement and critical review over the years has been of more *value* than you know. I also thank the NRC Book Talk group. Our sharing of good books, good talk, good wine and food, and friendship is part of what I do.

Thanks and love to my mother, family, and friends for all your support throughout this and other journeys. My love and deepest appreciation to Don Gustafson, to our five sons, to their wives and best friends, and to our *grand*children. You've been with me every step of the way.

Introduction

There is no Professional Development without Personal Development

The focus of this book is on teachers' personal and professional development. It is about teachers' learning, hopes, desires, struggles, and their instruction. The book shows what these things look and feel like from inside the lives of effective teachers and in their classrooms.

Often it is dissatisfaction or a personal/professional goal that moves teachers to become more knowledgeable. In the process of learning to teach, teachers experience personal growth and change. Personal and professional development are inseparable, for there is no teaching change without teacher change.

Among the most valuable experiences that lead to improving teaching are those of tension. Tensions arise during the complex process of working with children on a daily basis. In trying to help children learn and help themselves realize their professional and personal goals, teachers find that they are growing uncomfortable and need to change. This realization can happen quickly or over time.

Students in classrooms contribute significantly to teachers' learning and growth. Many times it is one child's struggle or a teacher's belief system about children's educational rights that signals a need for action. This book focuses on nine teachers' background and everyday classroom life. These teachers show their learning, growth, challenges, and rationale for change.

The classrooms in this book are diverse. The children are from rural, suburban, and urban areas. Their language patterns reflect a variety of cultures and geographical locations. The classrooms include average and advanced children, children of poverty, those who struggle in literacy learning, and unique learners who are often hard to reach. The teachers in this book are also diverse and unique. They are of either European or African descent. Some have won teaching awards and some have not, some are well published and some are not. All are professional educators.

The teaching in this book offers illustrations of effective practices in a variety of elementary classrooms. The teachers featured speak openly about their own struggles in learning to teach and how they became more reflective and knowledgeable, more confident, and more satisfied in the classroom.

JoAnn Archie, Andrew Allen, Karen Morrow Durica, John Greenwell, Jack George, Kris Gregory, Ruth Heil, Donna Ware, and Phyllis Whitin represent lifelong learners who are at early, mid, and late periods in their careers. They work in different places, including Pennsylvania, Colorado, Kentucky, Georgia, New York, South Carolina, and Canada. Yet, their personal and professional development has universal commonalities. All played a vital role in creating their own learning experiences. Their learning has happened and is happening, in a specific "place." That is, cognition (learning of all kinds) is situated in particular physical and social contexts; it is social in nature, and it is uniquely distributed across individuals and groups.

What It Takes To Be a Teacher provides insights on issues that are vital in understanding and supporting ourselves as human beings and professionals. The book addresses questions such as these:

- What kinds of resources and experiences do effective teachers draw upon?

- How do these resources and teachers' roles coalesce in professional development?

- What are some of the factors that help teachers acquire and sustain a positive journey toward effective teaching?

- How does this feel and what is it like to find one's place in the profession?

I have always wanted to know more about the personal and philosophical aspects of learning to teach. Having been a classroom teacher and a teacher educator, I thought there was a missing piece in teacher education and professional development. In education we focus on what teachers should *do* in the classroom, and this is good. Teaching is remarkably complex; thus teachers must be highly skilled (McIntyre and Pressley 1996). However, we also need to focus on how they should *be* in the classroom and how they change and grow. Learning to teach is an intimate affair at the most theoretical and practical levels. A great deal of teaching knowledge and its development is tacit and must come to light in order to clarify this thing called lifelong learning. Becoming a professional educator can be a lonely trek; if not understood on a personal level, it can remain unaccomplished by many well-intended teachers. The best investment in children's learning is in their teachers' learning. Thus, it's essential that we engage with the lived experience of those becoming effective teachers. The purposes of this book are to provide that engagement and to

- Show the challenges teachers face when they work on building their knowledge and searching for their own strengths—these essential elements of effective teaching are captured in their professional and personal development journeys.
- Show the centrality of informed experimentation in the classroom, the critical need for healthy classroom communities, and the supreme value of learning to let the children lead us to better practice.
- Show the power of teacher inquiry and the necessity of research-based teaching and provide access to effective instruction for teachers, child-centered classroom management, and instructional conversations with children.

To more clearly understand what it is like to do professional development, I began to search for effective teachers who were interested in talking about their personal and professional development. I found JoAnn Archie, Andrew Allen, Karen Morrow Durica, John Greenwell, Jack George, Kris Gregory, Ruth Heil, Donna Ware, and Phyllis Whitin by talking with friends about effective teachers, by meeting them at conferences, and by knowing about their publications or teaching awards. As I talked with these teachers and read about their experiences and their philosophy, I came to know and appreciate the contributions they had to make.

1

Understanding the Ways Teachers Learn

PENNY FREPPON

I taught second grade and as a reading specialist and art teacher grades one through six. I taught in public schools in low-income urban neighborhoods with a majority of white Appalachian and some African American children. I currently teach at the University of Cincinnati in the College of Education's Teacher Education and Literacy Program. I've lived in northern Kentucky most of my life.

The purpose of this book is to show personal and professional development co-occurring through the experiences of real teachers in practice. This group of elementary teachers, JoAnn from Kentucky, Andrew from Canada, Karen from Colorado, John from Kentucky, Jack from New York, Kris from Kentucky, Ruth from Pennsylvania, Donna from Georgia, and Phyllis from South Carolina, was brought together to provide insights into

- how resources and teacher learning coalesce
- how specific factors help teachers acquire and sustain positive and well-informed journeys toward effective teaching
- what it feels like to learn to teach and belong in finding one's place in the profession

In this first chapter, I highlight the resources and specific factors that effective teachers use in their personal and professional development. In the next five chapters the teachers and I discuss these topics in greater depth as well as what it feels like to learn to teach. These chapters show the teachers' philosophies, changes, struggles, and actual practices in the classroom. They show the inseparable nature of personal growth and change and professional development. A discussion of the social nature of teachers' personal growth is beyond the scope of this book. However, the teachers and I believe that the social strongly mediates the ways in which teachers and children learn and what they learn.

Attributes of Effective Teachers

All the teachers in this book engage in interior, reflective dialogue, read professional books and journals, attend conferences, and are inspired by other educators. Through these means they transform their learning and reflections into improved classroom instruction. The teachers' development clearly shows a strong sense of social justice and the understanding that teaching is a moral endeavor. Such attributes of good teaching have been described by Ayers (1993). Ayers (1993) and Graves' (2001) research shows that as in all professional practice, teaching requires energy and dedication. This energy and dedication becomes self-sustaining when it is supported by

- teachers who are principled people
- teachers who have a strong sense of responsibility for student learning and motivation
- teachers who search for their own strengths
- teachers who long for enjoyable interactions with students and have an abiding compassion for them (Ayers, 1993).

Interior, Reflective Dialogue

I've chosen interior, reflective dialogue as the starting point because this source is very important to teacher learning and because reflective practice is highlighted throughout this book. Teacher reflection is not new; it is a familiar refrain in a great deal of literature. However, the content, human experience, and role of reflection in actual instruction is often a mystery. Reflection is not a complete description of what is happening in effective teaching. Reflection is not (educational) reflection unless it is linked to teaching action. Reflection involves conflicting thoughts and questions. It is hard work and it can be painful. It's a dense and not well-understood concept and process (Rosko, Vukelich, and Risko, in press). Acting professionally on reflection requires true grit.

Reflections from Three Teachers

Karen, Donna, and Jack's reflections are captured in the following discussions.

First, Karen Morrow Durica shares her interior dialogue and shows the impact that struggling learners have on a principled teacher with a strong sense of responsibility and the strength to see her teaching through a critical lens.

> Adam, an endearing fourth-grader, entered my classroom reading at least two years behind his peers. That year I tried everything I knew to help: non-fiction books that "matched" his interest, recognition of his efforts, and praise for his work. I smiled and thanked Adam's mother when she thanked me for his best year ever. I knew I had helped him, but I knew also that in my heart I had not helped enough. The student I wanted to help most, I could not help enough. I thought a lot about why. I had not connected Adam's home life with schoolwork, I wanted to be so student-centered but I did not allow much self-selection, and I "covered" the curriculum much too much. In Adam's year I vowed to find a way to make sure none of the bright and trusting eyes of my students would reflect the pain I saw in his eyes.

Next, Donna Ware reflects on how an abrupt and oppressive change in administration prompted a powerful phase of self-examination and questioning. Donna is a constructivist teacher. She is a person who holds the theory that all learners construct their own knowledge through meaningful interactions. Donna had a literature-based classroom until she clashed with a new principal who did not approve of her philosophy. It was through this dark and lonely period that Donna moved decisively toward learning to teach.

> I taught in a school with a wonderful principal, Dr. McNair. There I developed teaching skills and curriculum that I was proud of. Sadly, Dr. McNair was transferred and the new principal and I clashed badly. He demanded that I change the way I taught and I felt as if part of *me* had been ripped away. With the climate of our school changing almost over night, I experienced physical and psychological distress. Fortunately, in keeping with my school-teacher grandfather, I had learned to keep a journal. Writing became my therapy during this very difficult period.
>
> *Journal entry:* I go home at night with headaches and tensed-up back muscles. I'm not the only one feeling this way. If I were, I would really believe I was losing it. This new principal has a strong need for control. I'm not use to this; I'm used to acting on my own. I think most of us here (at school) are. We are used to being independent teachers with good ideas. We are not being given the chance to work up to our potential.

Looking back on this entry I wondered about our children in the classroom. When we exhibit strong control over them, do they not also go home with headaches and tense backs? I believe this is so.

Donna missed living by her principles and being kept from the enjoyable interactions she had had with her students. She was angry and very frustrated. These powerful feelings and her reflective habits helped Donna find a solution to her problems. She left her school and joined the faculty of another that she knew had a philosophy in keeping with hers.

Jack George's reflections on his previous teaching life tell the tale of a teacher who realized that he had to embark on a search for his own strengths and those of his students.

I taught for a long time in a large inner-city system that served low-income children from diverse cultures. There I experienced no flexibility, and to my lasting sorrow neither did my students. The classrooms were quiet, "the blinds were straight," the students were quiet. I kept excellent grade and attendance records and my reading lessons were so carefully scripted I could split the sixty-minute block into three perfectly timed twenty-minute segments.

Group I (Bluebirds) would be in oral-reading flight with me while Group II (Hawks) fluttered hopelessly in the workbook, and Group III (Robins) pecked away at the mandatory backup worksheets. I have no idea how I kept my sanity. I even caught myself falling asleep when daily oral reading proceeded in lockstep manner.

True, I was comfortable because there was *no* challenge or risk. But, I felt less and less content, and the pebble in my shoe grew to boulder size. Finally, in utter frustration I tried a few new things with my students and saw a remarkable change in them and in myself. So, I applied for a new position and got the job in a new school! After a long, dull, and dead-end journey, I truly began my professional and personal development.

To learn and grow, Jack had to search for his own strengths. Above all, he had to find a context that supported his journey.

Learning from Professional Books, Journals, and Conferences

Learning from books, journals, and conferences is critical for personal and professional development. Study after study shows that reading the literature, conferring with colleagues, and taking teacher-education courses help sustain lifelong learning. Many states now require more postgraduate work, and universities and colleges across the country are improving the quality of these courses. Without teacher learning classrooms become dry and barren places.

Three other teachers, Ruth, Phyllis, and John, provide examples of how they experienced their learning and avoided barren places. Ruth Heil's journey highlights the necessity of a search for one's own strengths. She speaks first.

> I went in search of that missing piece—something that would define a place where children were more personally involved and where I was part of the (classroom) community instead of just a disseminator of information. I read Donald Graves' book *Writing: Teachers and Children at Work* (1983) and was so amazed that I read it again. While trying to implement his method of writing with children, I had no one with whom to share what I was attempting to do. I needed further guidance in using writing workshop and writing process concepts in my classroom. What a challenge! I attended my first National Council of Teachers of English conference. While I was at a Donald Graves' session, I talked to a person sitting next to me about my struggle in teaching writing. This woman (who turned out to be Carol Avery, former NCTE president) suggested I attend a summer writing program. I did, and it was the catalyst for changing my whole way of teaching. My teachers were Nancie Atwell and Mary Ellen Giacobbe. Not everyone can have such fine teachers, but everyone can read these authors. Through intense growth periods and times of isolation and doubt, I concentrated on learning through my students and others. I read the *New Advocate* (children's literature), *The Reading Teacher,* and *Language Arts.* I attended conferences. Through it all I had to sift through a myriad of possibilities, assess again and again, and—in the end—I made my own informed decisions.

In Phyllis Whitin's case, some wonderful university experiences stand out as critical to her personal and professional development. These courses and their instructors appealed to Phyllis' teaching principles and her affinity for math.

> A class taught by Dr. Deborah Stone at the University of New Hampshire inspired me to love mathematics. She ignited her students with a playfulness toward math, whether it be answering the attendance roll with a "different number name for twenty-four" than any other class member or appreciating the mathematical dimensions of children's literature, such as *Four Fur Feet* (Brown 1990). She led us in explorations with manipulatives, and for the first time I truly understood the concept of place value. With my classmates we learned to appreciate numeration systems that have been invented

by diverse cultures across history. For Dr. Stone, mathematics was not a set of mysterious absolutes but a functional tool for making sense of the world.

For John Greenwell, professional reading has always been an important element of good teaching practice. Teaching theories and child-centered practices interest John. The reasons some teachers select one method and philosophy while another teacher makes a completely different choice is intriguing. In searching for a "right" way of being and teaching in his classroom, John knew what he didn't want. This is the kind of thinking most teachers' experience. John didn't want any part of "assembly-line" education.

While working in his master's program, John came across a program called Foxfire (Wiggington 1986). Reading more about the program and understanding the research that supported it made him realize that this was the philosophy he had been trying to hone. In his own words John describes his experience.

> In the early stages of teaching and searching for my "style," I discovered an incredible program called Foxfire. It's based on John Dewey's idea that children learn best from their own experiences. The program originated in a high school in north Georgia. Essentially, it gives students the authority to direct their own studies based on their own interests. Generally, students write and read a great deal about their communities. Learning then expands to other areas and dimensions outside the students' communities.
>
> I found this culturally-based program attractive. The approach seemed to be what I needed to polish my desire for a democratic and student-based classroom and teach in more consistent ways. However, I had some reservations. I taught very young elementary students, not young adults in high school! Could younger students be trusted to direct their own curriculum? What I soon discovered was that with my guidance students could develop engaging curriculum that was interesting and exciting for them.

Learning from a Sense of Justice and Understanding Teaching as a Moral Endeavor.

In addition to using the resources discussed previously, utterly fundamental issues such as learning from a sense of justice and understanding teaching as a moral endeavor strongly impact teacher learning. Research on these issues is at last coming into its own, with many articles and books written for and by teachers (see Allen, 1999). The voices of three representative teachers show how childhood and adult experiences contribute to their journeys toward good teaching. JoAnn begins this final discussion, followed by Andrew and

Kris, who also began teaching with similar concerns for the social and cultural aspects of children's learning. Listen to JoAnn Archie.

> When I arrived at my first teaching job on the first day, a large bus was sitting in the parking lot. The principal announced that we were going to visit the inner-city neighborhood from which some of our students were bused for racial integration. As an African American I knew then this principal was a wise woman and that many eyes would be opened. In the neighborhood we walked the children's walk from the bus stop to their homes. Many teachers could not veil their astonishment or embarrassment as they glanced at front porches with refrigerators and other appliances. I watched as some created smiles in greeting parents who opened their doors.
>
> Why had I not responded to the conditions of poverty in the same way? Was I a better person? Not at all, I just happen to live in the community; I have all my life. From my perspective the conditions we saw were just a way of life.
>
> The following week, our faculty took a different field trip; we walked through the school's home community of poor and working-class white families. Now, it was my turn to stare in amazement. I had never visited a rural, low-income trailer park or a farm with a creek in the backyard. I realized I had my work cut out for me in teaching these children from a different community than I knew. As Moll and Gonzalez (1994) have shown us, we must build on the experiences and strengths the children bring. Trying to blend (and do justice to) complex life experiences of inner-city children and rural children would be a tough job for a first-year teacher. I knew I would have to enter my classroom with an open mind and heart.

For Andrew and Kris, childhood experiences fed their desire and determination to improve instruction. Their comments speak to the moral imperative for teaching that respects all children and shields them from shame. Andrew Allen begins:

> My earliest school memories are painful. On the first day of first grade we were to write our full names. I gathered my courage and told my teacher I didn't know how to write Andrew. She seemed angry and looked hard at me as she printed my name in huge letters across the board. I was able to copy them and can still see each letter as if etched in my mind.
>
> Later, I became what was considered to be a good student. I was quiet, did what I was told, and knew the teacher was in charge. I learned to be passive, I didn't like school—it was something I had to do.
>
> Those early experiences made me determined to find a better way. Teacher education provided it. Through a more humane way of teaching

and my affinity for literature-based instruction, I learned that both students and teachers could have a hand in their own learning. I wanted to develop ways to sustain engagement, enjoyment, and satisfaction in learning. When I became a teacher, I wanted my class to be different, certainly much different than my own had been.

Kris Gregory's voice completes this section with a brief discussion about early experiences that led her to become an effective math teacher. Painful memories set in motion her sense of responsibility and passion for a morally just practice.

> Sitting in the first chair of the first row, feet dangling because I was small for my age, I found that mathematics instruction meant that the teacher stood at the blackboard and imparted her wisdom to us in the form of endless equations on ditto sheets. I still remember the distinct odor of the chemicals and the damp feel of the work sheet paper in my trembling hands. Because of the way I was taught, I both feared and loathed the subject. Thanks to my dad and my math-literate friends, I made it through school. As I entered the field of teaching I vowed that I would find a better way and never be the kind of teacher I had in school. Teaching has to be more than imparting skills. It must take on providing a just classroom community in which children's learning is respected.

A personal search for the socially worthwhile and morally just career is clearly part of the knowledge of good teachers (Ayers 1993). For each teacher in this book and ultimately for all effective teachers, this theme is of utmost importance.

Five Principles of Effective Teaching

As noted previously, several theoretical strands ground the professional development of Ruth Heil, Karen Morrow Durica, John Greenwell, Donna Ware, Jack George, Kris Gregory, Phyllis Whitin, JoAnn Archie, and Andrew Allen. As you will see in subsequent chapters, these principles are inherent in the instruction the teachers have developed on their teaching journeys. In Tharp, Estrada, Dalton, and Yamauchi's (2001) principles of effective teaching provide a framework for understanding what actually happens in effective instruction. These principles include

1. joint productive activity in which teacher and student(s) produce together
2. language development across the curriculum

3. contextualization by making meaning that connects school to students' lives

4. cognitive complexity that teaches complex thinking

5. instructional conversation—teaching through conversation

Each of these principles has multiple themes or examples of effective teacher-student interactions. These principles and themes were generated also by the Center for Research on Education, Diversity and Excellence (CREDE). This work stands with many other fine researchers:

- the work of Katherine Au and her colleagues on teaching and learning with children of diversity and those who struggle

- those interested in language learning and thought, such as Vygotsky, and motivation researchers, including Guthrie, Wigfield, and Oldfather

- experts in reading comprehension and writing, including Calkins, Clay, P. David Pearson, and many others who have provided invaluable work on theory and research

- Duffy and Roehler, Palinscar, and Winograd and others who are concerned with the nature of good practice and psychologists such as Bruner, Bandura, Rogofff, Wertsch, and Wittrock, who study class-rooms and community learning

These excellent researchers are representative of the many fine contributors in the field. Tharp and his co-authors help reveal the underlying complexities imbedded in effective teaching.

For the Instructional Conversation

At the end of each teacher's section are interactive questions and ideas for instructional conversations. Using the questions and ideas as or after one reads these sections will support in-class or in-group and out-of-class projects. The questions and ideas are to be used only as a guide that facilitates your work. There are many creative things that can be done with each section. Be imaginative!

The two categories in the instructional conversation are in-class or in-group thinking, writing, and talking and reflective thinking and action. The categories are designed for course instructors to use during in-class discussions, for preservice and in-service teacher study groups, and for participants and leaders of profession-development projects. The first category is useful for sparking immediate discussions. The second category is useful for fieldwork.

To conclude this chapter, here is some information on up coming chapters.

The Teachers and Their Expertise

The teachers in this book have many areas of expertise, and they integrate all the language arts throughout their practice. Each teacher also has an interest in writing. The next four chapters are organized around the teachers' personal journeys of growth and development and their instructional foci.

Chapter 2, Reading Comprehension and Instructional Inquiry, *Ruth Heil, Karen Morrow Durica, and John Greenwell*

In addition to detailing the unique change and growth experiences of Ruth, Karen, and John, Chapter 2 demonstrates sound reading comprehension and inquiry teaching.

Chapter 3, The Writing Process, *Donna Ware and Jack George*

This chapter brings to life Donna Ware and Jack George, who consider writing instruction to be at the center of their practice and a force in their growth and change.

Chapter 4, Writing in Math and Science, *Kris Gregory and Phyllis Whitin*

These teachers describe their professional development and personal affinity for math. Their classroom instruction shows the power of writing and problem solving in children's learning mathematics and science.

Chapter 5, Building Community and Teaching with Respect, *JoAnn Archie, Andrew Allen, and John Greenwell*

This chapter focuses on the unique personal and similar professional goals for managing the classroom. These teachers live in United States and Canada.

Chapter 6, Personal and Professional Development:
A Lifelong Process, *Penny Freppon*

This chapter focuses on some of the salient aspects of the book and raises issues for future discussions.

For the Instructional Conversation

In-Class or In-Group Thinking, Writing, and Talking

1. Read the forward written by Bill Ayers and the preface. Then list
   points from both that resonate with you. Connect several points with
   something you believe or something that has happened to you. Read
   aloud or post three points you would like to discuss with someone in
   your group. After discussing, move on to one more person and talk
   again. Share what you learned or a question you discovered in these
   conversations.

2. Examine the list of Ayers (1993), *To Teach* and that of Tharp, R.,
   P. Estrada, S. S. Dalton, & L. A. Yamauchi (2001), *Teaching Transformed*. Engage in an "Easy/Hard" exercise. List the attributes and
   principles in two columns. Match pairs of Ayers' attributes and
   Tharp's principles, by drawing lines from one list to the other. Meet
   with a peer and discuss which are easy or hard to accomplish.

3. Discuss how your thinking on some topic (exercise, family, diet, vaca-
   tions, etc.) has changed or developed over your lifetime. Write a short
   response and discuss it with someone near you. Identify causes or im-
   petus for change and compare and contrast your thoughts.

References

Allen, J. 1999. Class Actions: *Teaching for Social Justice in Elementary and
Middle School.* New York: Teachers College Press.

Ayers, W. 1993. *To Teach.* New York: Teachers College Press.

Brown, M. 1994. *Four Fur Feet.* New York: Hyperion Books for Children.

Graves, D. 2001. *The Energy to Teach.* Portsmouth, N.H.: Heinemann.

Graves, D. 1983. *Writing: Teachers and Children at Work.* Portsmouth, N.H.:
Heinemann.

McIntyre, E., & M. Pressley. 1996. *Balanced Instruction.* Norwood, Mass.:
Christopher Gordon.

Moll, L., & N. Gonzalez. 1994. "Lessons from Research with Language-Minority Children." *Journal of Reading Behavior.* 26 (4): 439.

Rosko, K., C. Vukelich, & V. Risko. In press. "Preparing the Reflective Teacher of Reading: A Critical Review of the Professional Education Research." *Journal of Literacy Research.*

Tharp, R. & P. Estrada, S. Dalton & L. Yamauchi. 2001. *Teaching Transformed.* Boulder, Colo.: Westview Press.

Vygotsky, L. 1978. *Mind in Society: The Development of Higher Psychological Processes.* Cambridge, Mass.: Harvard University Press.

Wiggington, E. 1986. *Sometimes a Shining Moment.* Garden City, N.Y.: Anchor Books.

2

Reading Comprehension
and Classroom Inquiry

WITH CONTRIBUTION BY RUTH HEIL,

KAREN MORROW DURICA, AND JOHN GREENWELL

This chapter features three teachers' professional development and their classroom practices with reading comprehension, early intervention with struggling readers, and inquiry-based instruction. In the first section you'll meet Ruth Heil and see how she learned and developed in her teaching of reading comprehension in a regular elementary classroom. Next, Karen Morrow Durica shares her personal and professional journey with a reading intervention program. John Greenwell's work concludes this chapter. He discusses his growth and development and the ways in which he conducts inquiry instruction in a multiage primary classroom. Although this chapter emphasizes reading, notice that Ruth and Karen fully integrate writing and talk in their instruction and that John's inquiry teaching also incorporates all the language arts. The practice of all three teachers shows the inseparable nature of personal and professional development.

Ruth Heil: *Instruction that Promotes Children's Independence and Reading Comprehension*

Ruth has had a long career in preschool and primary teaching. For the last twenty-plus years, Ruth has taught in a rural Jamestown, Pennsylvania, school. The school has about 350 students, primarily from working-class families, with some families on social support.

"Are we almost home?" This was my often-asked childhood question, and its affirmative answer led to feelings of comfort and security as my family

Ruth Heil

completed one of its Sunday afternoon car trips. In reflecting on a teaching career, I am filled with thoughts of being almost home—sure that I'm on the right track in teaching, but always open to finding additional ways of working with children to help them develop into skilled readers and writers. When I retire I want to feel a sense of accomplishment knowing that I have enjoyed and endured the journey, and have kept my focus on children. I want to be able to say, "Home at last!"

Lucy Calkins spoke at a National Council of Teachers of English conference about what we do as teachers to support children in order to allow them to compose their own reading lives. In considering my own professional development, similar questions have developed for me: How have I created my teaching life? What are the factors that supported and influenced its growth? What experiences have affected and nurtured me personally and professionally to enable me to support my students, as they become involved with texts as readers and writers?

Although I did not consider these questions in my early teaching days, I urge others do so; it will enrich your life and your work. Now I know that such questions allow me to scrutinize my life as an educator. I hope my story will help beginning teachers and others develop their careers. Through experience, I can pinpoint episodes that have paved appropriate paths, although they seemed at the time just ordinary aspects of the day-to-day job. Major changes have occurred in the way I work with children, and I've been actively and intentionally involved in these developments. This seems to be a critical key in teaching: ongoing intentional reflection and action. It's work, but it's worth it.

My purposeful involvement in changing my teaching grew out of dissatisfaction with the manner in which my students were responding. To illustrate I will briefly share what happened in my search for my own strengths and those of children.

Armed with a degree in early childhood, I spent a decade teaching preschool children, including directing a Head Start program. Children's stages of development were honored; activities were planned using their growth and needs as a guide. Vivid memories of those preschool years recall magnificent block buildings and whole cities children constructed, some very complex with elevated highways, ramps, tunnels, and skyscrapers woven together. Children talked about their creations and asked me to write signs for their buildings, "Pam and Nicole's city . . . look, but don't touch." They were learning the power of written language.

My degree in early childhood education and my teaching with those delightful children helped me to sustain a developmental strand that I wove into my *disposition for teaching*. This disposition later helped me maintain a balance between theory and practice. I learned over time to stay student-centered and not content-centered.

When I moved to primary-grade teaching, keeping the student at the center proved to be a difficult task. At first teachers' guides, although helpful in some respects, seemed to dominate what and how I taught. After participating in reading and writing graduate classes, I was drawn more toward student inquiry and the use of children's literature. This personal attraction became the magnet, returning me to a student-centered approach. An animal research project discussed next provides an example of my approach.

I want to preface my discussion on the animal research project that follows by saying that this project was coordinated with the science curriculum. In the language arts' period I focused strongly on reading comprehension and writing.

In working with another teacher, I learned much from an animal project we did together. In this project we used a process and an animal research checklist that I adapted from one Nancie Atwell used in her middle-school teaching. We hoped the process would increase the children's confidence in pursuing the individual research project in which they would engage. We used many written language strategies and oral language events to increase the children's opportunities to learn.

We modeled the process by working through the checklist and learning about one animal together as a whole class. From the choices I presented for our project, the children chose an earthworm (in part, I suspect because we were reading Roald Dahl's *James and the Giant Peach*.) Here is an outline of how we taught after the children had chosen the animal they wished to study.

- Make an earthworm web that includes such categories as food, habitat, and so on.
- Meet with small groups of children to list ideas on the KWL chart (Ogle 1986).
- Share and list as a class what the children knew and wanted to know, which would come later after reading.

In this project, we searched for simply written series books such as *The New True Books* (Children's Press), *Rookie Readers About Science* (Harper Collins), *Let's Read-and-Find-Out* (Harper Collins), and *Eyewitness Junior Books* (OK Publishing, Inc.). All these books are very good for science and social studies. As we began, we did the following:

- We read about earthworms, took notes, and told others what we had learned about our invertebrate before beginning to write—we wanted to be experts.
- We wrote a first draft without our notes. In later drafts, we strove to include thoughts and feelings about earthworms.

As teachers we learned as much as the children and dealt with many problems in helping all the children participate in the whole-class earthworm project. Each child's participation was especially challenging as the class moved into individual animal inquiry projects, and we were grateful to have a two-teacher team. Brown-eyed and curly haired Chris is a prime example of the children with whom we needed to work.

Chris desperately wanted to learn how bees make honey, but his low reading level meant that someone would have to read to him. Here is how I helped Chris.

- I repeatedly read a book about how bees make honey.
- I recognized that Chris excelled at drawing and found that by drawing a diagram of the process, he was able to report to others how bees accomplish honey production.

By doing these two things I provided the scaffolding for Chris' weak area and emphasized one of his strengths.

All children need help of one kind or another, and in his case, Chris needed an extra amount. Things worked out. Chris experienced success and participated along with his classmates, and I was able to do some additional explicit instruction.

Research and Theme Cycling Combined with Developmentally Appropriate Instruction

During the years that the children participated in the animal research study, one goal remained constant: To help them pose questions, find answers, and comprehend what they read about an animal. By providing many opportunities to question and share that information in a variety of ways before they write a draft, they don't get into the habit of copying information word for word from resource texts. To this end, our research guide, or Animal Research Checklist (see the Appendix), has evolved to its current form.

Even though I was able to help Chris understand the honey-making process, there were often other children who needed assistance. In some years with larger classes, there were too many students for me to help. It was frustrating! Out of necessity, I made a change to working in small groups. Teachers gathered simply written books, magazine articles, etc., for each group's animal, so there was a variety of information available. Small-group work often provides the individual help a specific child needs, which might have solved Chris' honey dilemma. In developing their animal pamphlet, the group would have valued his artwork. I have also used paraprofessionals or aides and volunteer parents to help.

Our extended animal research integrates both language arts and science. Research-based minilessons are conducted, e.g., I review questioning techniques previously learned from interviewing parents about family holiday customs.

The question process requires more complex thinking and investigation. The question What does an earthworm eat? is more thought-provoking than Do they eat? (Yes, there are third graders who asked that question!) It's challenging for young children to develop strong information questions. As I struggled with this aspect of the research process, Donald Graves (1989) clarified my thinking and provided a more important goal.

> Some children have to do two or three formal reports before they have a sense of how to choose a subject and how to formulate effective questions. There is no need to rush to help children succeed. Rather, *a tone of discovery, sharing in community, and a sense of wonder about the information is what the teacher seeks to foster in children* (author emphasis). The process of learning how to learn—to formulate questions, read, and find an area of knowledge unique to oneself—eludes a majority of students over a lifetime.

I remind myself that these young students are just at the beginning of learning how to learn. That the squeals of excitement, yearning that children have for learning, and the discovering of something "awesome" is to be highly valued. Their own reporting skills and voice in writing come if we value the discovery they experience.

Theme Cycling

I team-teach in a third-grade reading workshop that includes lots of book reading and writing activities. We focus hard on reading comprehension. One strength of our workshop is theme cycling. Within this structure, children read and reread books and other materials on the same topic and engage in classroom discussions.

A goal of theme cycling is to teach children how to learn and teach others about the content they are reading. This instruction integrates varied and flexible activities *and* explicit instruction. Here are some key ideas to use in theme-cycling instruction.

- Make time for rereading: rereading scaffolds children through a developmental period needed to move to fluent reading.
- If beginning readers are struggling, don't move them to more difficult texts—in rereading they reap the rewards of fluent reading. The "feel of reading and comprehending" is crucial for success.

At the heart of it, theme cycling is inquiry, which cycles through some or all phases noted here. This teaching technique raises children's consciousness and gives them a framework for organizing information. This structure is all-important for children, especially for those who need additional support. Many researchers and teachers advocate theme cycling and these goals (Rhodes and Dudley-Marling 1996; Lipson and Wixson 1997). This way of teaching is tried and true.

Here are some steps or phases of theme-cycling instruction.

- Help students make a topic selection. Topics can be whole-class or small-group selections.
- Children's literature, field trips, and spontaneous classroom conversations and events can spark topics.
- Show students how to find and use resources on their topic. Resources include a variety of materials, photos, public information such as maps, flyers, and articles, library and classroom items, information from home and families, and books.
- Identify authentic ways of representing the information that is gathered (e.g., children can make posters, give talks with props or artifacts, draw, make webs, or write papers and stories).

Two essential things to remember in planning and conducting theme cycling are to (1) make students' active involvement a top priority, and (2) make ongoing lists of concepts, materials, and ideas.

Begin with small steps you can handle—for example, a small group and a limited number of resources and ways to represent the information children gather. You will have a greater sense of how these guidelines and concepts play out in the classroom as you read about my classroom and later as you read about the work John does with inquiry in his multiage primary classroom. In my discussion, I focus primarily on how I use theme cycling as a way to teach reading.

"Grandparents" is an example of one of our children's favorite theme cycles. Our goal is to help students understand and appreciate their own grandparents and older people in general. In addition this project nudges them along in their reading development! We also offer opportunities to see how authors depict grandparents in various texts. (See the reference list at the end of this chapter.)

I often begin this project with *Knots on a Counting Rope* (Martin 1987). It's a heartwarming story of a grandfather helping his blind grandchild grow to become independent. After reading and listing the characteristics of the grandparents and discussing the story, the children take home lengths of yarn and tie a knot in it each time they hear a story from a grandparent, an older relative, or friend. These personal home stories provide rich material for the children to share with their classmates and highlight the importance of family involvement and oral language in children's lives. The children return with their yarn and choose to share one story during small-group time. Some extend their oral storytelling with a drawing before they write. Many stories are funny or poignant, as shown in the following example.

MY PAP GROWING UP

When my pap was six years old, he came to America from Croatia (Yugoslavia). I think he had to sail on a boat for fifteen days. He talked in Croatian. All they ate were apples. The apple sellers spoke their language, so that's why they only ate apples.

They sailed to New York where their father met them and brought them to Pennsylvania. About one month later, he and his brother entered first grade. They couldn't speak any English. When the teacher asked pap and his brother to go up and sing a song, they sang it in Croatian. Everybody laughed at them and they had to put their noses to the wall. They were punished. He and his brother were embarrassed.

By, Jenny

After Jenny read Allen Say's *Grandfather's Journey* (1993), the story of a Japanese immigrant who traveled back and forth between the United States and his homeland, she said, "My grandfather never got to go back to Croatia. I wonder if he wanted to have us see it too?"

Reading Comprehension

I follow the theme-cycling study with two weeks of independent, self-selected reading infused with minilessons on reading and writing strategies and skills. I conduct the minilessons prior to children's independent reading periods.

To learn how to plan the lessons, I talked daily with my student readers and writers. I learned what to do through these talks and by following the district language arts curriculum. Talking with students showed me the way. I shared strategies that writers use to tell their stories. I had "danced around the fringe" in reading workshop and knew we had to be more intentional in addressing this question: What strategies do good readers use?

I wanted the children to become aware of what helps readers make meaning of their texts; that is, I wanted to demystify the process so that they could become more self-reliant. The children and I began a running list of strategies that we kept posted in a visible spot in the room. At first, the only strategy the majority agreed on was that to become a good reader you needed to practice and read a lot. This is an important first strategy, but there is more that a reader can and should do.

To teach reading strategies better, I watched for opportunities within the workshop setting. One day, I made an observation out loud about a problem that I had observed readers encountering as I listened to them read. By making explicit that several readers were having the same difficulty, I was able to show students that reading is a problem-solving process. My teaching also encouraged independence as I explained the following to the class:

> Today there were several children who asked me words they didn't know. While asking me about a word you don't know is fine; it's not easy for me to do when I'm conferencing with others. If you stop to ask someone a word every time you don't know one, it's hard to get meaning from what you're reading. Let's brainstorm a list of other things you do as readers when you have a word you don't know.

We created this list together:

1. Sound it out.
2. Ask someone.

3. Skip it; read further to see if you get an idea from the other words in the sentence.

4. Use Step 1 and Step 3 to try to find a word that makes sense.

5. Look at the pictures.

6. Use a dictionary.

7. Skip it, write it down, and look it up later.

I was impressed; this list showed me again just how much young children can do. I then asked them to pay attention to what they did during the next ten minutes of silent reading and asked them to record their responses in their notebooks. Many of the children found this difficult to do. Most of the children said that they didn't miss any words. In talking further with some, I discovered that it was hard for some to take their focus off the story and concentrate on the process of what they were doing. Some children also were hesitant to indicate that they didn't know a word because it might give the impression that they weren't good readers. Because it was early in the year, I understood that a sense of trust was still in the making. I had asked them to do something for which they weren't ready. Most of the children said that they sounded out the word or asked someone. Often they could decode or say the word but didn't have a clue to its meaning.

These early observations and discussions led me to do a series of minilessons designed to inform the children of two important things:

- that all readers encounter unknown words when they read
- that there are ways to try to read the word or read around the word so that you can still get meaning from the text.

These minilessons also enriched the children's skills in selecting books that more closely matched their reading levels. Each year, I tailor my examples to fit the children in that class. (This keeps me on my toes *and* from getting bored.)

I began the series of minilessons with a discussion of different levels of reading materials and how they might vary for individual readers.

I used samples of books written in increasingly difficult ways—for example, from easy picture books to chapter books with longer sentences and more complex vocabulary. We categorized the books:

- *Easy* texts, in which you can read all the words, e.g., *Frog and Toad are Friends* (Lobel 1970), *Little Bear* (Minarik 1957)
- *Just-right* texts, in which you know most of but not all the words, e.g., *Miss Marlarkey Doesn't live in Room 10* (Finchberg 1995), *Rotten Ralph* (Gantos 1976)

- *Challenge* texts, in which you might need assistance to really understand, e.g., *Blackberries in the Dark* (Jukes 1985), *Help! I'm a Prisoner in the Library* (Clifford 1979)

For all children, there is a fine line between these categories, which can be set only by individual teachers and children's standards. All children need support in learning how to decide categories for themselves as their literacy increases. We have learned over the years how really hard it is to find books on a traditional third-grade level, because intangibles such as children's interest come into play. Word recognition matters, but it is not all that matters. The children and I talked about how hard it is to get meaning by yourself from books when you miss too many of the words.

I hoped that this discussion would quietly discourage some of my students whom I know struggled as readers and had chosen harder chapter books because it was prestigious with their peers. I also guided these struggling readers to a certain amount of reading at an appropriate level while respecting their interests. This move made me more conscious of their interest in an unexpected way.

Linking Children's Interests to Varied Genre

As integrated reading and writing events were geared to children's needs, lessons and interactions led to further learning and growth for me. For example, one fall semester Mickey asked me about information books, and I noticed that he and others seemed hungry for books about the environment, particularly about animals. For awhile, I kept track of book genres children selected during their library time. I noticed that most of the boys invariably signed out books about sports, animals, or science. This observation helped me to see that my primary-grade focus on fiction and stories was too limited. I increased the number of nonfiction books in my classroom and read some research on the importance of a variety of genres in the primary classroom. Later on, I found I could keep track of patterns of library selection in my head. I used those mental notes to keep the classroom library updated.

Students' Collaborative Reading

Science or environmental books invariably have vocabulary that is beyond my third-grade readers, but such books are rich with pictures and content and are wonderful to share with a friend. This presented an interesting problem. I carefully observed two boys, one of whom was a reluctant reader. Chad found it hard to stay on task during silent reading. He wanted to talk and sometimes distracted students near him. I worried about Chad, a child I saw as ripe for troubles with learning and getting along in school. Chad's pal, Bob, was a popular student. I allowed them to work together; these two boys spent time devouring and discussing the pictures and parts of the text in a book about ponds and rivers. I listened as they wove their experiences into a book discussion.

- Chad reads the word *bullhead* (a mean-looking creature). He describes it as a dragon fish and tells Bob, "It's flat enough to hide under a stone" (observing illustration).
- Bob, who swims in a pond near his home, replies in alarm, "I ain't going swimming no more in my underwear." Both boys laugh.
- On another page they wonder about why the backswimmer (a water bug) spends most of its time upside down. Is it a good way to get away from an enemy, or play dead?
- On another page Chad remarks, "Wow look at those pretty flowers." He tries to read, M, m, m, m and Bob lends a hand, "Marsh Marigolds." Both boys nod in agreement.

These two children's interactions led our class to adjust our book categories, and we created a new one we called challenging, but good to share with a friend. I made sure our class knew that I learned about this new book category from Chad and Bob, and this increased their status and provided many opportunities for them to work together. Thus, they could enrich their mutual support for learning. Chad's and Bob's wildlife immersion shifted from *Pond and River* (Parker 2000) to a poetry book about insects. They recited many poems from *A Joyful Noise: Poems for Two Voices* (Fleischman 1988) and wrote one of their own patterned poems modeled on Fleischman, "Book Lice" (Figure 2–1).

Teaching Reading Strategies at the Right Time for the Right Reasons

While my students engaged in silent reading, I talked with them individually and listened to them read for short periods of time. I compiled a list of issues around which I might create minilessons. For example, when Kayte read, she bubbled over with experiences that she connected with the story. I noticed,

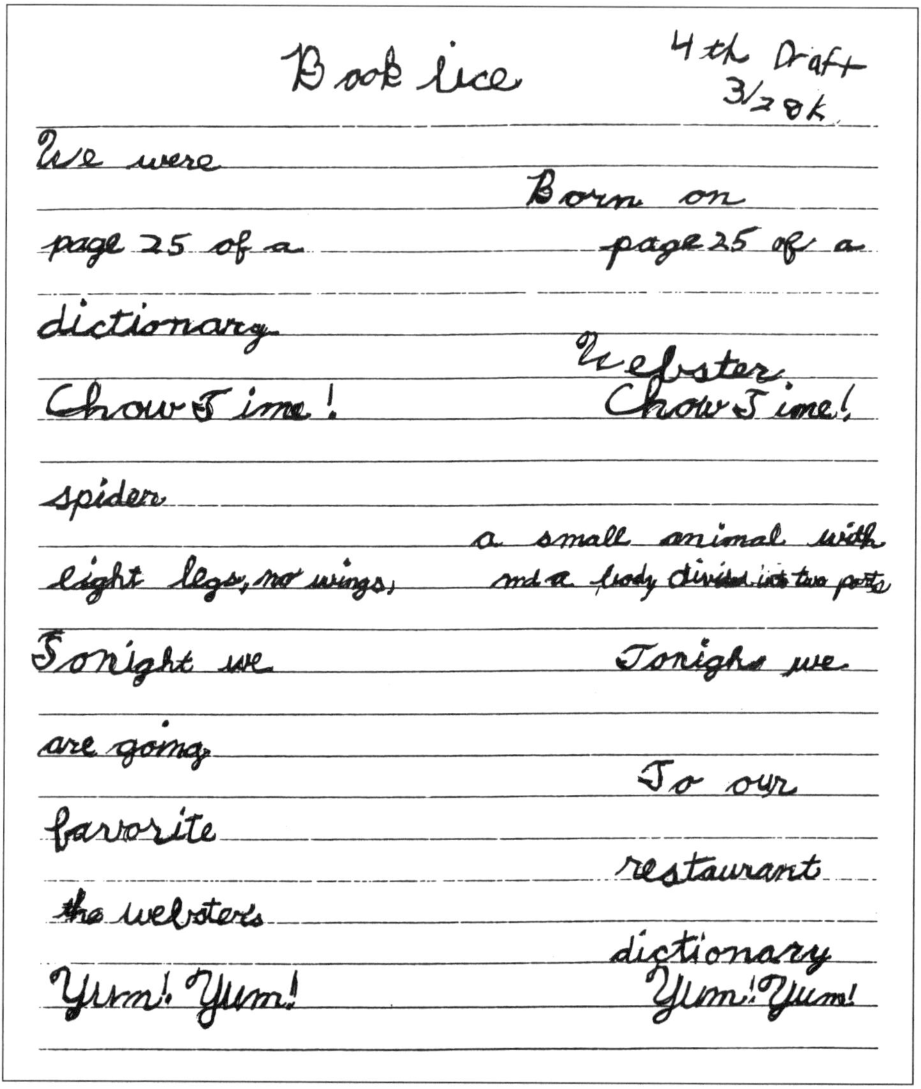

Book lice   4th Draft
                         3/28k

We were
                    Born on
page 25 of a   page 25 of a

dictionary.
                    Webster.
Chow Time!   Chow Time!

spider
                    a small animal with
eight legs, no wings,   and a body divided into two parts.

Tonight we   Tonight we

are going.
                    To our
favorite
                    restaurant
the websters
                    dictionary
Yum! Yum!   Yum! Yum!

Figure 2–1.   *"Book Lice"*

however, that she often omitted word endings, which at times affected the meaning of the story. Kayte helped me become more aware of this problem with other children.

It was also good to observe my students' physical involvement in reading. Kyle pointed to each word while his head bobbed up and down in time with his pointing finger, as if he were reading a list. We used a marker to help him keep his place, and then I asked him to look at several words before reading aloud. What a difference! Kyle read smoothly and with expression. A minilesson on "chunking" soon followed, because I knew several children were word-by-word readers. By far the most prevalent problem in word-by-word reading was the variety of things children did when they were stuck on a word. Some tried to decode and some stopped dead. As a class, we worked our way through several of lessons in order to model what they might try when they got to a word they didn't know.

Samples of Reading Strategy Instruction

Minilesson: Reading Strategies

In addition to our class discussions of reading strategies, I needed to provide explicit demonstrations, so I adapted a cloze procedure. I used two paragraphs on an overhead that I had adapted from the book jacket description of Balthwayt's *Tangle and the Firesticks* (1987). I gave the background of the story and asked the children to read the first paragraph in which I had covered a word (mischievous) except for the first letter. I suggested that the students read past the unknown word to the end of the paragraph. Then I instructed, "Go back to the sentence with the unknown word, read it again, and ask yourself what word begins with *m* and would make sense in this sentence." The most popular word the children selected was the word *mean*. In a second example, I gave the same directions for the word *clumsiness*. The word *clothes* was most often guessed. The examples were:

> Of all the little people in the north woods, Tommy is far and away the most *mischievous*.
>
> He doesn't mean to get into trouble, but this is how he ends up—in trouble.
>
> As tiny Tommy was running away from mother fox, he dove into a hole in the ground. It was the Fire Cave! No one is allowed in the cave. Someone said, "Don't you know the rules? You can't come in here. Your *clumsiness* could have put the fire out. I'm going to tell on you."

We talked about these two predictions of unknown words and how some children would know the words and some wouldn't; it was a very individual situation for each child. The emphasis was, however, that we could use phonic clues *and* context clues. Importantly, we discussed how to look beyond the first letter and analyze the word. We also discussed how to bring more and more thinking about the story to the problem of unknown words and how one's personal experience with the word might be of assistance as well.

Minilesson: Proper Nouns

I observed that many children got into trouble when they came to an unfamiliar proper noun. This showed me I had to do some teaching. I devised a paragraph for the overhead that would help children understand that they could read for meaning even though there were several proper nouns to decipher along the way.

The directions were to read the selection and to say "blank" when they got to a name that was unknown. During the second reading, I asked the students to try quickly to say a name that looked or sounded something like the word in the selection. If they wanted to read the paragraph a third time, they could. When they were ready, I asked them to write in their notebooks what they thought the paragraph was describing.

I watched a few of my struggling readers look absolutely stumped. I circulated around the room, encouraging them to try again, and slowly, most of the children really began to dig in. Here is the selection.

Pablo and Rosita are from Guadalupe, Mexico. They came to the United States with their mother and father. They moved to the big city of Roanoke, Virginia. Tomas and Marguerite, their parents, have always wanted to live in America. Many of their friends have moved to this country to the Appalachian Mountain area, which is like their home in Mexico.

My primary goal was to support the children's attempts to make sense of the text, even when confronted with many proper nouns they did not know. Most of my children knew the words Mexico, United States, and Mountain, so I thought they could make sense of this passage using the strategy I was teaching them. (See Figure 2–2.) As with many passages we read, if we emphasize meaning, we can check on the unknown words later. This is an especially important strategy for children in content reading (social studies and science). We don't have to decipher *all* unknown words at the moment we are reading (I don't). I also stress vocabulary instruction, but the strategy in this minilesson is important. It builds independence and confidence. For young readers who are still word-reading, something like this paragraph really throws them off. Talking about these situations really helps children become more persistent in trying to understand what they read.

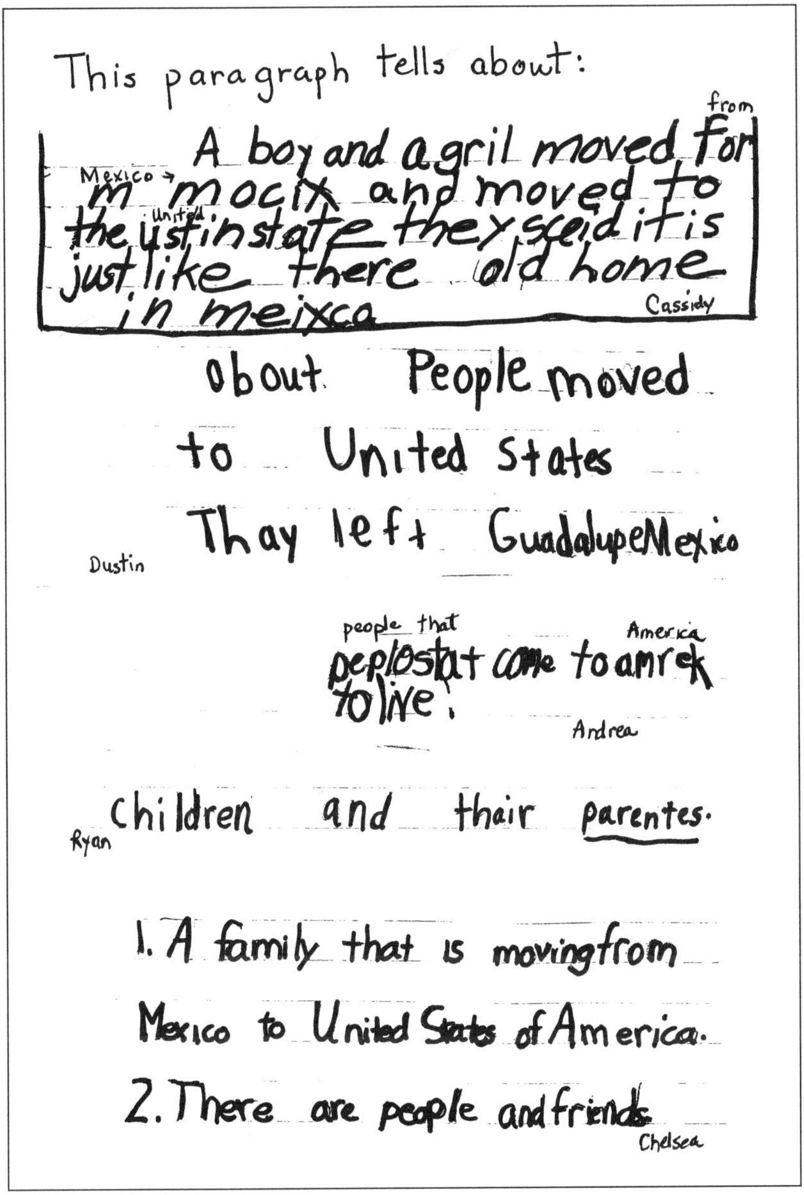

This paragraph tells about:

from
A boy and a gril moved for
Mexico → m mocix and moved to
United
the ustinstate they sceid it is
just like there old home
in meixca
Cassidy

obout People moved
to United States
Thay left GuadalupeMexico
Dustin

people that America
peplostat come to amrek
to live.
Andrea

Ryan Children and thair parentes.

1. A family that is movingfrom
Mexico to United States of America.
2. There are people andfriends
Chelsea

Figure 2–2. (*continued on page 28*)

This paragraph tells about
A girl moves from Mexico.
to America their mother and
father. They go to
Virgina. It has lots of
mountains. The mountains
remind them of their old
home.
                                    Klistiny

This pargraf is about

differt   culter.

A little bid said

I what to move to

Amrca with my frainds.

The kids parnts allways

Kayte Whant to live in Amaca.

This paragraph tells about

a family who lives in the U.S.A.

that was from Mexico,   meagan

Figure 2–2.

After each of these two minilessons, we spent a little of our reading time each day for a week compiling examples of what strategies we used as readers and then shared them with the class. Here is an example of a student's effort to understand her text. Allison was reading the poem "In the Graveyard" from *In a Dark Room* (Schwartz 1991). She did not know the word *corpses*. She looked at the pictures (that were key in this case) and reasoned, "There are three dead bodies, so that word must mean dead bodies."

Although there often were times the children could not say or understand the unknown word, I saw them make progress using the process we had discussed. For example, Sean was reading Marc Brown's *Arthur's Halloween.* (1982) He read:

> The only one Arthur recognized was the Brain. He was wrapped in aluminum foil. "I'm a baked potato," said the Brain.

There was a picture on the page; however, Sean didn't know the word aluminum. In his notebook Sean commented:

> "I read past it. I knew foil. I looked at the picture. I tried to sound it out, but it didn't make sense. I kept reading because I wanted to find out what happened."

Sean's involvement in the story gave him enough information to get the general idea; his interest in the story spurred him to move ahead in the text.

Following these experiences using various strategies to unlock unfamiliar words, I asked my students to respond again in their notebooks to what they now did as readers when they got to an unknown word (Figure 2–3).

I have come to realize that by third grade, most students have internalized the phonetic system and that this is an invaluable tool. I find, however, that more children need the kind of strategy lessons that I have just described. From this instruction, they learn to persist and combine strategies such as the use of phonetics and meaning making. When using more than one strategy and engaging with print deeply, children become stronger readers in mind and spirit. Occasionally, however, there is a student for whom phonics instruction is important at the third-grade level. This year I have a student, Cory, who has been in so many schools that he has missed much vital reading instruction. The Title I reading instructor is working with him on aspects of the alphabetic system he doesn't know. I listen for his use of phonics and other strategies when we have a reading conference and teach him accordingly.

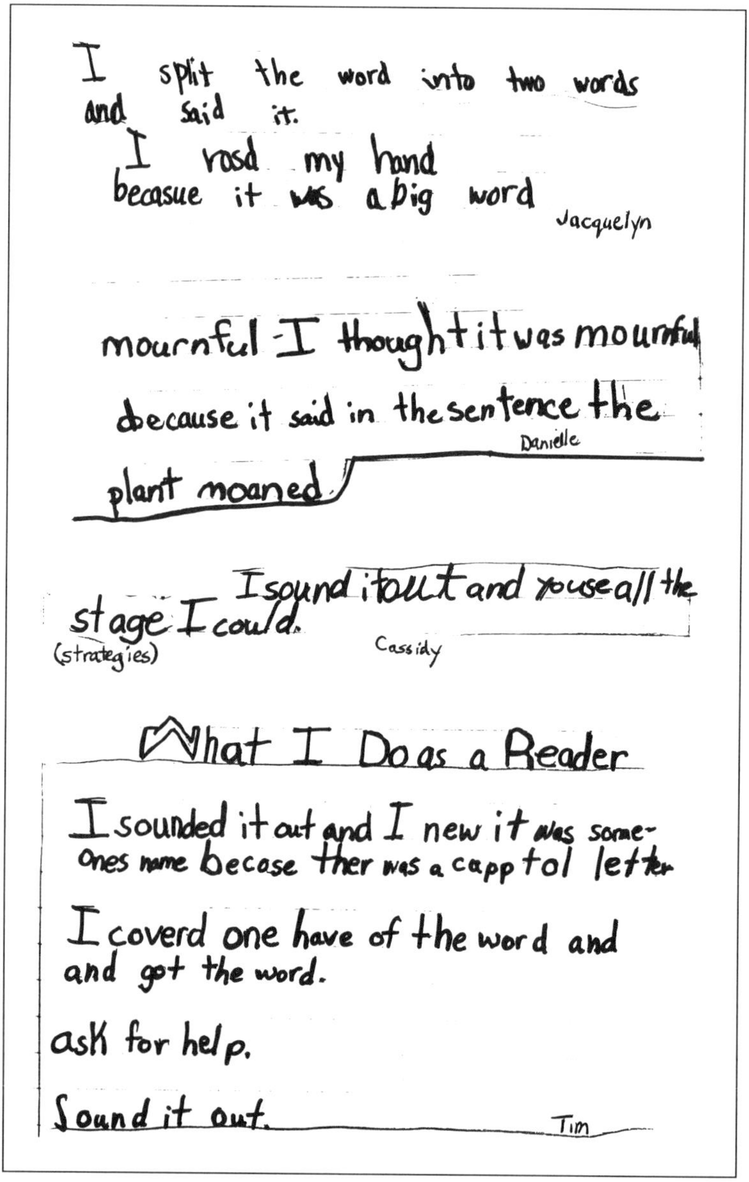

I split the word into two words and said it.

I rosd my hand becasue it was a big word

Jacquelyn

mournful I thought it was mournful because it said in the sentence the plant moaned

Danielle

stage I could. I sound it out and rouse all the (strategies)

Cassidy

What I Do as a Reader

I sounded it out and I new it was someones name becase ther was a capptol letter

I coverd one have of the word and and got the word.

ask for help.

Sound it out.

Tim

Figure 2–3.

As a culminating activity to the lessons described previously, the children received a card to keep in the back of their notebooks that included all their suggestions for unlocking unknown words.

More Teaching and More Projects

Recently, the children in our classroom started bringing in toys from home. This became a distraction. To respect their interests and keep an orderly environment, my coteacher and I set aside time for children to bring in a collection that represented a hobby (sports cards, dogs, stuffed animals, etc.). The children met in groups to share and discuss their hobbies. With my coteacher's and my help and drawing from their hobbies, they developed a list of vocabulary words. What a wonderful list of words we had! I find I can always learn to teach better when I let the children show me the way. Learning to be open to them and still incorporating curriculum can be difficult, but it is an essential lesson for teachers. I have experienced much joy in the progress children make toward becoming self-reliant readers.

In our classroom, we are all learners and teachers. This does not mean that all problems have been solved, but it does make problem-solving easier. My own growth rekindles my love for working with children. My work with children in the context of their lives opens doors for me to help them compose their own literate lives. The bottom line is that I know a one-size-fits-all approach will not meet the needs of my third-grade students.

Conclusion

We teachers nudge children toward becoming risk-takers, and we must heed this lesson as well. It's most improbable that I would have changed as I have if I'd not been willing to become knowledgeable about research on children's learning and research on teaching. The stumbling blocks I encountered stymied my progress at times, but in the process I found my teaching self and became reenergized for the task. Through the children's reading and writing and their enthusiastic responses, I came to know them and develop a strong sense of a class "family." Personally, during the last twelve years I have become a reader, a writer, and a researcher. This personal and professional development is extremely satisfying. Glenda Bissex once said at an NCTE conference session that researchers are always "hanging around the margins." Since I found my teaching self, I think you'll find me in the margins—observing, learning, and adapting.

For the Instructional Conversation

In-Class or In-Group Thinking, Writing, and Talking

1. Ruth seems like a fulfilled person. How important is personal fulfillment to you? Write quickly on this question and discuss it in a small or whole group. Then do a quick write on your views of the importance *or* inseparability of personal and professional growth. Discuss this second issue.

2. Ruth discussed some key points in her changes in learning to teach. Review her direct statements and read between the lines to see what you infer from her writing. Note a few ideas on paper and share them with someone who shares her or his paper with you. Combine your ideas into one list and identify the things on which you agree and disagree. (This can also be done with other teachers, such as Karen and John in this chapter.)

3. Ruth notes that by third grade most children have internalized the phonetic system. Discuss this statement in small groups and try out the following questions.

   • Given the context, what do you think Ruth means by her statement?

   • Do you agree that most third graders have internalized the system?

   • Does phonics instruction link with other essentials such word learning and spelling? If so how?

   What values do you find in the way Ruth approaches the animal research project with her third-graders? Can you connect these values with those in Chapter 1?

4. Generate a theme or topic for a theme-cycling project. Brainstorm with a partner and list the ways in which you would include math, science, social studies, and all four language arts. Discuss your ideas with the group.

Reflective Thinking and Action

1. Ruth has intellectual roots in early childhood education. Examine the position statement of the National Council of Education for Young Children (www.naeyc.org) on developmentally appropriate practices. List Ruth's practices that match the position statement. Or, list your own practices in your or a colleague's primary classroom and follow the same procedures. List practices you believe should be included in

classrooms beyond preschool. Use research to support your conclusions in a short paper or oral presentation.

2. Several authors, such as Glenda Bissix, Lucy Calkins, and Rhodes and Dudley-Marling, are noted in Ruth's section. Locate an author of interest. Read this book and report on it by using the author's points that connect with issues you've had in your own classroom or seen in others. The report can be written or presented in a minilesson or vignette that helps demonstrate your meaning.

3. Read five grandparent books listed in Ruth's reference list. Using one or more of these books, develop an inquiry project appropriate for your intended or actual grade level. Share the project with others. To extend this project implement it with children in a classroom or another place. Report on teaching the project to your peers or another teacher.

4. Read more about reading strategies such as those in Hagerty's *Readers' Workshop: Real Reading* (1992) or those of Harvey and Goudris (2000) in *Strategies That Work.* Plan a minilesson for a small group of readers with a common need. Prepare copies to share with your peers and a discussion of your rationale and goals. Use your own understanding and something from Ruth's discussion that you find of value.

Karen Morrow Durica: *An Early Reading Intervention Program for Children Who Struggle*

Karen Morrow Durica teaches in a middle-class elementary school in Littleton, Colorado. This school includes children from low-income families. Karen has taught as a classroom teacher and engaged in teacher leadership and professional development projects. Karen's focus is on her personal and professional growth and on early reading intervention program for struggling readers.

I have always loved to learn—and I have thought of teaching, like life itself, as a journey and not a destination. This simple idea has supported my development as a teacher and as a human being.

So many people and experiences are woven into the tapestry of my memory and supported my affinity for learning. My parents made an incredible impression on me. My mother was a highly intelligent woman who loved school and excelled at her studies. Yet, as one of eleven children, at sixteen

Karen Morrow Durica

years of age her contributions to the family had to be financial. In spite of her begging to continue with school, her father informed her that she had to go to work. My mother never received that cherished high-school diploma, but she was my source of knowledge and ideas all her life.

Then there was my dad. He was also from a family of eleven children, but his father went to "seek his fortune" when the youngest sibling was six weeks old. It truly was up to the older children to support the family. So dad left the one-room schoolhouse and worked in a coal mine in Pennsylvania at the age of thirteen. He never returned to school, but his passion for reading and his gift of listening filled my childhood with the knowledge that books could teach you anything you wanted to know. Dad never rewarded me or my five siblings for good grades, nor did he punish us if our grades were down. However, through him we came to know that to go to school was a blessing and that in school, nothing but one's best would do.

In addition to my parents' inspiration, I had teachers I'll never forget. In seventh grade my teacher read to us *The Red Badge of Courage* (Crane 1976). I went to school even when I was sick so I wouldn't miss a chapter of that incredible tale. Then there were my tenth-grade geometry teacher and my college biology teacher, who made me work harder than I ever had in my life but gave me smiles, encouragement, and a sense of accomplishment that remain with me today.

I received a degree in education from a small, rigorous liberal arts college, and by the time I did my student teaching I felt confident and ready to go. I taught the first four years in first grade. Though overwhelming, it was a wonderful adventure. I adored the children but I struggled—especially with record keeping. There were forty-eight (yes, forty-eight first graders!) math papers and phonics papers as well as that many other assigned papers to work though every night. I did bulletin boards monthly and had a principal who checked my lesson plans every Monday morning. I wondered if I'd ever have a life outside my classroom. Yet sprinkled among all the mundane activities I felt were so necessary at the time were moments of children laughing, singing, and learning. There were brilliant tooth-missing smiles, goodbye hugs, and a sense that I was doing something truly important.

Oh, the mistakes I made. I taught isolated phonics lessons straight from the manual and assigned the designated worksheets to every child. I had only ability-grouped reading lessons; everything was directed by the sequence of my manual. I cringe at the thought of it. However, because I loved books I read to the little ones and they often wrote their own stories based on these books. We read poems and painted, and at these times our room was alive with the excitement of learning. I sensed even then that I was doing more for the children's literacy in the "extracurricular" activities than I was in my lessons. I was frustrated. I knew deep down that there had to be a better way. I was not yet ready to make the needed moves, but I knew that I had to learn more. In time I learned through graduate work.

At first, I was terrified of returning to school; it had been fifteen years since my undergraduate degree (having taught and taken some time off for my three children). I consciously thought about the need to take risks and took the plunge. Graduate school changed my life. With each successful completion of a course, I became more aware of the importance of success in the lives of my students. From that point on I was convinced that children's beginning literacy learning had to be successful. I've never given up on this idea.

An Era of Trials and Tears

As a regular classroom teacher from first to fourth grade, I have helped many children learn to read. But there were also times when I could not help a child because I simply did not have enough knowledge and skill. At times I had to retain a child, as I did one year in first grade.

As the children filed out of my room on the last day of school, I thanked them for being such good teachers. I had learned so much. About two-thirds of the thirty students I had were fluent readers, more than ready for second grade and beyond. Six were beginning readers with all hopes of continued success, and two were strong emergent readers who just needed support, encouragement, and informed teaching to grow. Armed with the summer lessons I wrote for their parents, I felt these two would do fine. But there were two other children, Gabe and Charles, who—in spite of my focused instruction and hard work—remained emergent readers unable to grasp basic reading strategies and learn sight words. They told stories from pictures and could use letter or sound cues to decode some words. I thought at the time that phonemic awareness was a part of their knowledge base. However, these two young children did not *use* this knowledge when they read. They could not manage even simple preprimer texts. Their writing indicated semiphonemic understanding, and they were in fact representing only the beginning and ending consonant sounds of some words. There was no early intervention at my school at that time. And, despite all I had done and because of the promotion system in place, I had to retain Gabe and Charles.

I knew that retention was not the answer. The failure to be promoted is so painful, I believe it affects a child for life. Research shows that retention contributes significantly to the dropout rate. Children quit school when they feel out of place with their younger peers and simply grow tired of the struggle to succeed.

Having faced the tragic situation of Gabe and Charles more than once, when my district began an early reading intervention program, I jumped at the opportunity to learn more about helping young readers. Our early reading intervention program was based on Marie Clay's (1994) Reading Recovery procedures. At the time, this intervention program was limited to special reading teachers of our district. Unfortunately, I was not a special reading teacher.

Satchel Paige is credited with a marvelous saying: "Never let your head hang down. Never give up and sit down and grieve. Find another way." I had kept this saying on my classroom desk for years, and in this case, it had true meaning for me. I found another way by asking for a first-grade assignment the following year. I proposed to my principal that by taking the early intervention program training I surely would have a better grasp of first-graders' reading problems. She concurred and arranged for a teacher to come in and teach my students math so I could have the required thirty-minute one-on-one instruction with a student who would be part of my training.

Early Intervention and the Knowledge and Beliefs That Make It Work

As noted previously, Marie Clay's historic contribution was the foundation for our district's program. Clay's Running Record is an invaluable part of her research on reading. This assessment and teaching technique is highly conceptual and involves marking errors that children make in oral reading on the basis of the cueing system(s) they use. My interpretation of Clay's philosophy includes the following concepts.

- Teacher observations of what children do when they read are key to good instruction (rather than sole reliance on normed and other standardized tests).
- Effective teaching demands strong education, ongoing professional development, and, above all, a deep respect for children's capacity to learn.
- Effective teachers help children see that reading and writing are sense-making processes.
- Effective instruction builds on what children know and what they need to learn, with an emphasis on daily success and the steady introduction of more challenging reading material.
- Effective teachers include writing with reading as part of the whole of literacy and clarify the phonetic aspects of reading with struggling readers for a specific period in their early reading development.

Training in early intervention offered the framework I needed for effective literacy instruction. This framework is well grounded in a better understanding of reading and writing as language systems. Each encounter I had with a student was enveloped in and sustained by these beliefs. The framework of explicit teaching moves or protocol is outlined next.

- Have the child self-select a familiar book and specifically reinforce the things that he or she did well in reading—watch for strategies the child knows and those he or she needs to know and talk about them together.
- Take a running record of the child's oral reading with a new book and use the information to guide skill and strategy lessons.
- Encourage the child to write a sentence or two about the book he or she has just read and work on words that are not spelled conventionally.
- Use *Elkonin boxes* to help the student "stretch" hard words and support breaking the code. (See the Appendix for a sample Elkonin teacher/child conversation, an Elkonin box technique and a child's writing in the teaching protocol.)
- Conclude the lesson with a new book that will provide opportunities for the child to apply and extend his or her knowledge and strategies about reading.

Through the early intervention training I learned the importance of rereading familiar books and about the role of specific reinforcement. Learners need to know what they are doing right if they are to continue to grow. I like the metaphor Victoria Purcell-Gates (1996) uses about teaching a child how to ride a bike to show how early intervention and effective one-on-one instruction works. She notes that we use training wheels or actually run alongside a bike with our hand on the seat and handle bars in order to help the child ride and see how riding feels. The goal is to learn to ride without taking a fall and getting injured. This is an important goal in early intervention (and any good teaching). Although we do not teach without some risk, we strive to provide the support needed and keep children from getting hurt as we guide them toward more and more literate understandings.

I found that taking Running Records and spending many hours analyzing miscues provided me with insights into what was happening in the minds of my students as they interacted with texts. The collaborative writing we did during reading deepened my thinking and gave me ideas for the next instruction point. The following example shows how I scaffolded one child's learning and encouraged his independence in an early intervention lesson.

Early Intervention at Work

Timmy was my first intervention program student. With his sandy blond curls, his mischievous hazel eyes, and freckles sprinkled across his nose, he skipped his way into my room and into my heart forever. Here is an excerpt from one of our lessons.

KD: Good morning, Timmy, that's a great T-shirt. It has writing on it.

T: Yeah, it's my team, they won yesterday.

KD: Great. Did you have fun at the game? (Timmy nods.) I'm glad you brought your book back. Which one do you want to warm up with?

T: I'll read this one. Can I do this one too?

KD: You bet! (Timmy reads the familiar stories—the rereading/reinforcement part of the lesson. I then tell Timmy about good things I noticed in his reading. I make the reinforcement specific.)

KD: It's great to hear you laughing when Josh has the noodles on his head. When you got stuck did you look at the picture for an extra clue?

T: Yeah, I could see noodles on his head!

KD: Good. That's what good readers do. They also look at the letters and sounds in the words. Let's look at noodles. What do you see?

From here we discuss decoding while working on the word *noodles* and note that this is an important part of reading.

Timmy then reads a new book and I take a Running Record (Clay 1994). We talk about his strategies (what he did right), and then I make suggestions and coach him on using multiple clues to read. What I say depends on what Timmy needs right then and what I know he needs to learn in the future. I always aim for the child's long-term independence.

KD: How did you do with that book?

T: Good. I like it when it ends, "rain, rain, rain!"

KD: I could tell. Was there any place you needed work?

T: Over here. I can't get that word. I called it river—but I know it's not.

KD: Yes, river was a good choice at the time. It makes sense, but what's wrong?

T: It starts with *s*.

KD: Great, you know what to do to get hard words. (We continue and Timmy practices, with my help, to decode *stream*.)

We also draw around the letters in the word *stream* and discuss the meanings and spellings of the words *river* and *stream*. This lesson goes on to include Timmy's retelling of this book, some collaborative writing, and the introduction of a new book. The lesson ends with Timmy and me reading in chorus to help him get the feel of the new book, to experience fluent reading, and to end the lesson on a positive note.

In lesson after lesson, I watched Timmy grow into a child who not only could read and write but who also loved it! I watched myself learn and grow into a teacher who had a more solid understanding of how emergent readers attempt to make meaning out of print. I made a bookmark of the treasured note Timmy gave me at our last meeting. He wrote "I waz mad to red." (I was made to read.) In the years that followed, Timmy frequently showed me the book he was reading as we passed in the hall. When Timmy was in fifth grade, he saw me and waved his book in the air. It was the original *Jurassic Park!* He *was* made to read!

What had worked for Timmy? I spent time thinking about that. My conclusions supported what Clay professed and upheld my language philosophy: I was able to work with Timmy early in his literacy endeavors—long before he had time to form an image of himself as a nonreader. I had worked from Timmy's strengths; I had delivered systematic, explicit instruction that specifically met his needs; and I had scaffolded his reading to try to ensure his success and independence. Specifically, by careful observations of his miscues, I looked at his strategies, growing knowledge, and everyday needs as he read orally (see the Appendix for skills and strategies information). I kept urging his independence, but I did not let him experience the sting of failure. I checked for and taught according to his efforts and specifics crucial to reading success. I also used three guidelines from Marie Clay (1985) that work for young struggling readers.

- Read for meaning: Model how readers think and ask the child, "Does that make sense?"
- Focus on words themselves and make use of letter-sound relationships (decoding). Use meaningful words such as the child's name, those of his or her friends and family, favorite sports, or movie titles.
- Use the child's sense of language and what a sentence should sound like. Ask, "Does that sound like 'book talk' or the way we would say it?"

Timmy and I also did a lot of collaborative writing. Timmy decided what he wanted to write, and he spelled as much of each word as he knew. For conventional words or parts of words he did not know, I either linked what he knew to the unknown element or simply supplied the answer while noting for future reference where Timmy still needed to go. During our writing time, Timmy read and reread his conventionally spelled language. This strengthened the connections he was able to make between spoken language and written text. In the past, my students had read their own approximated spelling. But I learned that this complicated their ability to link reading to writing. In my experience, struggling students progressed better when they saw and studied their own words with the letter patterns in conventional spelling form.

I wish I could say that all my teaching stories have the same happy ending as Timmy's. They don't. An early intervention program is not a panacea, and it cannot operate in isolation. Factors such as parental support, consistency of instruction in the child's classroom, and unique individual development play decisive roles in the final outcome. Yet I am convinced that early intervention is significant in supporting struggling learners. I have seen children—those least experienced with print—come to think of themselves as readers. They can discuss books and strategies with the best of them. They have a long way to go, but they know they are going, and for the most part, they are enjoying the trip. These kids learn to read. There are few things as exciting, as humbling, and as rewarding as being present as a child moves from seeing "ants on a page" (Turner 1986) to words. It is a profound experience, and I have never gotten used to it. After many years of teaching, I still get a lump in my throat when I realize I am in the presence of someone who has just crossed the line to literacy. Crossing that line in safety with positive feelings is imperative.

Personal Growth as a Teacher

I began my story of personal and professional development by sharing that I have always loved to learn. This passion for knowledge, along with the experiences involved in implementing new skills and strategies, enables me to build on and sustain the "disposition for teaching" that is essential for teaching. I know what I believe about written language and how I apply those beliefs are core to the success of my students, not the materials available or a script in a manual.

In *Invitations,* Regie Routman (1991, 26) writes that effective teaching ". . . is not conditional on the materials the teacher is using; it is conditional on the teacher's theory of how children learn. It is the literacy model the teacher holds that determines the type of instruction that actually goes on in the classroom." It is my beliefs, not my manual that guides the decisions I make about books and lessons. My publication of *Literature Links to Phonics* (Durica 1996) was not only my effort to connect materials in emergent and beginning readers' classrooms to the broader picture of reading, it was also a profound self-assessment of how far I had come in my own understanding of reading and of how children become literate.

I believe more than ever in the benefits of early intervention. Success gives birth to more success, and I have made Don Holdaway's (1979, 12) statement my mantra: "If we continue to make literacy a criterion for basic dignity in our society, we cannot tolerate the failure with its poignantly modern forms of misery and maladjustment. [We] should either find a preventative solution or excuse a large proportion of children from school attendance."

For the Instructional Conversation

In-Class or In-Group Thinking, Writing, and Talking

1. This activity is called "Take a Stand." Write one belief about teaching or learning that you have after reading Karen's section. Then, gather in

small groups and have one person place his or her statement in the middle of the table. Each group member considers the statement and places a strip of paper near the statement to the degree to which he or she agrees with it. Placement near or on the statement means strong agreement, farther away denotes a question, or partial agreement, etc. Explain the placement to the group and discuss your views. The purpose of this activity is not to bring the group to consensus but rather to clarify and refine beliefs by examining multiple perspectives.

2. Karen says that the statement, "Never give up and sit down and grieve, find another way," attributed to Satchel Paige, means a great deal to her. What is revealed about her character in this statement? Brainstorm and list your responses individually, as a class, or in small group and discuss the list(s). Use the question What drives this or similar kinds of determination? in your discussion. Brainstorm and list your responses individually. Then discuss your list in a small group or a large group.

3. Devise you own thinking, talking, reading, or writing interaction. The only criterion is that you find ways of including every member of the group. If you like to create your own interactions, feel free to do so throughout this book.

Reflective Thinking and Action

1. Using Karen's discussion with Timmy, list the teaching strategies that she uses. This may be done by the whole group or as an individual. Get into small groups. Have the group draw lots that assign each person a teaching strategy. People drawing the same strategy may work together on becoming an expert on the strategy they have drawn. In a future meeting discuss the theory and teaching of these strategies in your small group. Discuss the groups' responses to this project.

2. The instruction in which Karen engages in her vignette with Timmy represents scaffolded teacher and child interactions. Brainstorm in a small group (or whole group) and generate a list of what you think is meant by the term *scaffolded instruction*. Identify specific places in which Karen is scaffolding Timmy's reading (see if you can distinguish between emotional and cognitive scaffolding). Ask yourself what makes this scaffolded instruction and write a short piece. Then review Tharp and Gallimore's (1995) discussions on teacher and child interactions that mirror scaffolding, such as warmth and responsiveness,

joint problem solving, intersubjectivity, staying in the zone of proximal development (ZPD), and promoting self-regulation. Make a list of these points and compare them to your own. Bring this comparison to the next group discussion.

3. Select any book that Karen mentions and read it. Draw your own conclusions about how this book contributes to your learning, and write a letter to a friend or school administrator about your conclusions and why you do or do not recommend it to others.

John Greenwell: *Teaching Inquiry in a Multiage Primary Classroom*

John Greenwell teaches in a small rural community on the western edge of Blue Grass country, where "southern leanings" significantly shape the culture. In John's school, most of the children are from middle-income homes, with some from low-income homes. The low-income children are primarily white Appalachians, an at-risk group in this area.

John Greenwell

On my quest for that first teaching job, I watched the principal peer at my application lying on his desk. I felt fortunate to have been called in for the interview just a week before school was to start. He seemed pleased with what I had to offer, which wasn't very much because I had just graduated with a B.A. in the spring of that year. But somehow I sensed that he might hire me. Maybe he recognized that I was an older student who had dropped out of college to "find himself" and thought I was mature. Or, perhaps it was the look of desperation on my face and my obvious fear of being out of work that appealed to him. I think he knew I'd agree to just about anything he might present. This principal wanted to know if I thought I could make a child-centered, social constructivist theory of learning work in the sixth grade. I nodded away as he spoke and said with confidence "Of course." It was the only thing that I could say if I wanted the job. After the interview, the principal assured me he would call me the next day. He did. I had the job.

I began teaching sixth grade with hardly a trade book to my name and only some notion as to what and how I should teach. Little did I know that later I would find myself teaching in a primary multiage classroom. In the discussion to come I'll touch briefly on my sixth-grade experience and my transition to primary multiage teaching through inquiry teaching.

Learning About Purpose

For many teachers, the first year of teaching is the toughest, and mine was no different. For every success that I celebrated, I dealt with twice as many failures. The search for my "style" kept me on a constant roller coaster ride. In that first year with its up and downs, I realized it was the trying times, not the successes, that strengthened my convictions to become a better teacher and, yes, a lifelong learner. As trite as this may sound, the hard times were critical in pushing me to think harder and increase my professional development for what was ahead.

I remember the first day of school of that first year. I didn't have enough activities planned for my students. I wasn't used to sixth graders (my student teaching had been with primary children). I found myself with a thirty-minute gap to fill before lunch. I promptly forgot all my teacher education at that moment and assigned the children to write about "my summer vacation." Honestly, I did this after all the years I was in school and hated that assignment. I got what I deserved. I was bombarded with whines and groans; a boy said, "I hate to write" and put his head down on his desk. His female peer announced, "We did this last year!" as she got up to sharpen her pencil.

At home that evening I thought about what I had asked the children to do. I knew that *I* had rejected the assignment as a student and that what I had done was in conflict with my philosophy and theory of learning. Students must have self-selection, options to work collaboratively, and—above all in writing and reading—a purpose. After some serious thinking I devised a plan.

The next morning I asked one of the kindergarten teachers about the possibility of my students becoming reading and writing buddies with hers. This teacher immediately accepted my proposal. Now, perhaps my students would have a purpose, an audience, and they would have options for collaboration, some of which would be self-selected. After talking and planning with my students, the kindergarten children joined us the following week.

After about twenty minutes of reading and writing together, the little ones returned to their classroom. I let the class know I was proud of how well they had worked. My students quickly began to discuss their pupils. They noted that some little buddies knew quite a few words, and some didn't "do too good." Sixth graders, Ben, Jenny and Aaron, suggested that they write books for the kindergartners, and we were off. The entire class pitched in and began discussing guidelines for the project. I wrote their ideas on the board and scrambled to keep up with them. Within minutes students had started — they wrote zany and more traditional drafts, helped one another spell and punctuate, and drew and colored illustrations. I happily stayed after school binding and laminating books.

My class shared the books and gave them to the younger children. The sixth graders were proud and exhilarated. A successful bond between the older and younger had formed, the little ones felt affirmed and special, and the older ones felt successful. Authenticity is the first tenet of an inquiry-based, student-centered curriculum.

Learning about Multiage Teaching

After my first year of teaching sixth grade, I learned about the Kentucky Education Reform Act (KERA) in my graduate classes. This reform act was passed in Kentucky as a result of a state supreme court decision that mandated equal funding in all public schools. At this time our state also initiated a major reform aimed at school improvement. Part of this reform was the establishment of multiage primary classrooms. Our school was beginning to restructure to comply with the new law. As much as I enjoyed teaching sixth grade by that time, I wanted to teach primary children. At the end of the school year I sought and got a new position in a first through third multiage classroom.

Goals and Beliefs for Primary Children

I am committed to using democratic principles in the classroom as well as to being a good teacher of literacy. I want my students to have input into what they study and how they go about it. My goal is to help students become independent thinkers and problem solvers, which are the hallmarks of learning and being democratic. This kind of thinking is at least a step toward the critical thinking and democratic education described by Edelsky (1994). Inquiry-based teaching helps me meet my goals and the needs of my students. Inquiry requires that children self-select and self-monitor. They need a good sense of independence to do this.

Helping my children develop independence did not (and still does not) come easily. I knew that students needed to make choices, and I tried to create authentic curricula in which they could work. But, I was leery of some of the choices kids might make if they were given more freedom. Let's face it, finding a balance between teacher guidance, explicit instruction, and children's independence is a challenge. In my early years of teaching, the children were allowed to make "little" decisions, such as choosing writing topics and selecting playground games, but I still directed much of what they did. I hesitated to provide opportunities for genuine student input into the curriculum.

Students Lead the Way

Fortunately, I had a bright student in my class, Don, who had insurmountable curiosity and a great zest for learning. While our class was in the midst of studying deserts, a topic I thought everyone wanted to learn about, he approached me with a request to study sharks. The two topics certainly didn't seem to be related, and I wasn't really sure how they possibly could be, so we talked. He told me that his mother was going to teach summer school and that she told him he could help her on a unit of ocean study. Don wanted time to practice. And, I couldn't deny him the right to learn.

I helped him to set up a center in which he could create a papier-mâché shark and read various books on sharks. Don's responsibilities were to participate in the desert work and to include the class in his shark project. What I found astounding was that Don agreed to the requirements, brought in books on sharks, prepared his lessons as well as any teacher, and allowed all students to participate in his project during their center time. I also observed that the children seemed to have retained more knowledge and interest in Don's lessons that they did in mine. I was a bit envious! But, of course, I was very proud of him as well. This episode with Don was a revelation. In spite of my intentions, I needed to *see* the importance of student coconstruction of curriculum in this new light. Not a bad lesson to learn from an eight-year-old! Don's lesson led me to explore further and put into practice the unique features of effective inquiry instruction.

Designing and Implementing Inquiry

As I learned to teach, I was introduced to a program called Foxfire, which is based on Dewey's (1963) theory that children learn best from their own experiences. This program originated in Georgia, and basically it gives students the authority to direct their studies based on their own interests. In the Foxfire approach, children write about topics in their homes and community. Foxfire worked well with our state-mandated reform and district requirements, and it fit with my philosophy of democratic education. I found the program attractive, but I had some reservations about how it would work at an elementary level because it was originally created for high-school students.

I found that I had to create experiences for my younger students by developing a framework and then supporting them in making choices within it.

Putting Inquiry into Practice

With my beliefs about a democratic classroom, the Foxfire project information, and the successful experience with Don's work on sharks, I was primed to do inquiry-based instruction. The students' decisions and our classroom curricula flowed from their initial experiences. When this concept was combined with experimentation and hard work, I was able to create an inquiring classroom.

I made notes on the things that needed to be done before an inquiry project could be officially launched. These are the points that were worked out in class discussions:

- Make suggestions for a field trip and support the class selection of a location.
- Discuss topics students might discover on the field trip that they could study.
- Upon returning to the classroom, prep and conduct a brainstorming session to generate ideas for small-group study.
- Provide guidelines for the small groups to follow during their studies.

After some initial suggestions on my part, our class planned a field trip the very first week of school to a state park that has a large fossil bed. After a discussion of the things we would see and do there, the children were asked to discover something that they would like to study on our field trip. We then visited this park, which had just opened its museum, viewed the displays, saw a film, handled the fossils, and had a picnic lunch.

When we returned to the classroom, we brainstormed ideas for individual or small-group study. Some of the areas of interest that came up were Native Americans, river habitat, and dinosaurs. We listed study options on the board and the children came to consensus—we would study Native Americans (inquiry studies can involve several topics; this one happened to do that). We listed what they wanted to study on the board:

- Who were the Native Americans who lived in our area?
- How did these people live?
- What kinds of fossils existed in this area?
- Did dinosaurs exist in the area long ago?
- What were the river animals?

As a class we created guidelines for what student products must be, including a written report. The result could be a short "fact book" accompanied by a mural or other picture or some kind of model or display. However, they had to begin with books. Many students selected partners, although some chose to work by themselves. With my reminding and guiding, the students remained highly engaged much of the time. I believe this was so because they chose their own topics for study. Had I said, "We're now going to study Native Americans," the interest might have been less or not there at all. I've learned that students' input and their self-selection is critical to their interest, motivation, and ability to work hard. Teacher control does not support active learning.

The first- and second-grade children in my class not only have input on what they'll study, but they also have opportunities to choose materials they might need for their research topics. Each spring I allow students who are returning to my class the following year to help order our supplies from the catalogs. They really love this work, and for them it's like Christmas in April. One year, one of my students wanted me to order an electricity kit. This child was very knowledgeable about currents and circuits, and he loved to invent. Seeing the potential of his desire and inclinations, I ordered the kit and put him in charge of it. For two years he instructed other students in "small clinics" on how electricity works and lent the kit parts to peers so that they could construct their own circuits. Almost all these students learned the basic concept of electricity. All I did was provide the catalog, trust students to learn, make sure they had the materials they needed, and give them opportunities to demonstrate their knowledge.

Setting Limits

Even though my students have input into what goes on in the classroom, there are "givens," and students understand what they are. Givens are those topics, subjects, or assignments that I, as a teacher, require based on school curriculum or what I might deem necessary for their further study. I work hard to incorporate these givens into the topics that the students select, such as the inquiry projects described previously. One example of a given in my classroom is that all students must know multiplication facts by the time they leave my multiage primary program. Perhaps some would argue that memorizing facts might not be important or necessary; however, I see the need and so do most parents of my students. Importantly, my students decide how they'll learn multiplication facts; given that responsibility they take more interest in their learning. I provide a variety of opportunities and experiences through games and hands-on activities in order to support them in getting the task done.

Another given in my classroom is that students read and write every day. Inquiry projects include written language such as child-written texts, books, brochures, or any other kind of print. Oral language is always part of the project, and most projects include children's art. As I watch children learn and develop inquiry sense and skills, I observe them learning how to make choices. Occasionally, of course, some children do not make good choices, but learning from mistakes is part of the growing up and learning through inquiry. To keep children moving in their development and to keep order in the classroom, I intervene readily and redirect as needed. Asking students to try another way is quick, to the point, and often very helpful.

Conclusion

Inquiry-based instruction doesn't just happen overnight. It takes time and effort from the teacher and the students. If a teacher wants it, then that teacher has to be patient with it. If your students have been trained (and I use this word deliberately) to sit in tight rows, to be quiet until called on, and to do teacher assignments, then that is all they will do. It will take time to help students move out of this way of schooling. With the careful implementation of inquiry-based instruction, children will do so much—because they want to do it.

When I stepped into my first classroom and felt uncomfortable with assignments I made, it wasn't because I didn't know what I was doing. It was because at first I didn't trust my instincts. My apprehension about my teaching was real, and thankfully, I recognized that fact. I had to learn to ask myself, If

I were a student, how would I like to learn about this subject matter? What would make it engaging and provide more learning opportunities? Children are natural learners and shouldn't be deprived of owning the curriculum.

Sometimes teachers say, "How do you address the curriculum with your approach?" My response is that curriculum is based on the content and the skills that children are supposed to know at any particular grade level. In examining the curriculum, one can see that inquiry-based instruction provides a clear path toward curriculum goals. Thus, we can have it all in our inquiry journeys—higher-level thinking; self-selection; challenging work; use of language arts, math, social studies, and science; and meeting curriculum expectations.

My journey toward becoming an effective teacher and a person who is proud of his work has not been easy. However, it has been necessary—I don't think one can be an effective teacher without being proud of one's teaching. For me professional development (being in a constant learning state and networking with other teachers) is the key in maintaining my commitment and building my expertise.

For the Instructional Conversation

In-Class or In-Group Thinking, Writing, and Talking

1. Are you attracted to John's inquiry approach? What are the most compelling things about it? What are the challenges for the teacher? What are the challenges for the children? Write briefly and then engage in a written conversation on these questions with a colleague or peer. Remember, in a written conversation one draws a vertical line down the middle of the page and with a partner (writing on the opposite side) writes on one side only. There is no talking as the written conversation takes place. Following this, discuss your thinking and points with others.

2. Locate an instance in which John solved a problem or made a positive change by watching or talking with children. How do you characterize this kind of teacher thinking? Provide supporting evidence from John's writing. Do this on your own or collaboratively; if you do it collaboratively, brainstorm on the question, make lists, and come to consensus or detail your differences.

3. John's inquiry-based instruction may be characterized by some to be nontraditional. With this in mind, why do you think some teachers might be apprehensive about engaging their students in inquiry stud-

ies? As a whole group or in a small group, brainstorm a list of advantages and disadvantages in inquiry-based teaching. Write quickly to flesh out the top two or three advantages and disadvantages. Work with a peer or small group to deepen your discussion on this topic and sketch out how inquiry-based instruction might be introduced and made to work in nearly every classroom.

Reflective Thinking and Action

1. Read a book or several journal articles on multiage classrooms. Describe the positive and negative aspects from your own perspective and that of the author(s) you are reading. Check for commonalties and differences; write a summary and prepare a short discussion about your findings that can be shared with others.

2. Develop a topic about which your (future or present) students would inquire. After making an informal outline of possible activities and materials needed, use what you've learned in this section and what you know from other resources so far to write up your response in a short paper you'll discuss with others. Address these points: (1). How would you incorporate elements of independent thinking, problem solving, and decision making for the students as they engaged in this work? Be sure to identify the students' ages. (2). How would you organize the students' work for differentiated instruction? Provide concrete examples and be as specific as possible.

3. John Greenwell's journey toward professional development brings up the topic of education for democracy. Read Carol Edelsky's 1994 article in *Language Arts* (see references). Or read any of the articles or books Edelsky suggests. Explore this topic and delineate what you discover in memos. Refine your memos so that you can make an informal presentation in your class or group. Presentation conversations may be in small or large groups.

Chapter Summary

The personal and professional growth of Ruth Heil, Karen Morrow Durica, and John Greenwell clearly portrays risk-taking. As with all effective teachers, they are the risk-takers today's world requires. In the information age neither teacher nor child can thrive via the transmission system or what Freire (1993) called the banking concept. Given what we know about how people learn, we can never go back to (or allow) classrooms in which children are seen as empty vessels to be filled with teachers' knowledge.

Lifelong learning is challenging. But, it is essential, enjoyable, and endurable as Ruth notes and the professional development of Karen and John shows. Risk-taking and lifelong learning are inseparable and complex. Teachers learn theory, and the strategies and concepts that come out of theory, and they practice. Without question the path to personal and professional development requires a practice that is grounded in teacher's everyday classroom research. The teacher's research is focused on the child's social, emotional, and academic growth. The effective teacher strives to understand what the child knows, what the child is trying to learn, what the child needs to learn, and how the child feels. As the teacher learns about the child, research-based instructional protocols (the thinking and action steps of teaching) are practiced in the dynamic of classroom life and children's development.

This kind of teaching includes at least transactions among new information and the instructional process, intellectual curiosity, and a sense of responsibility and commitment to each child. Ruth Heil, Karen Morrow Durica, and John Greenwell's practices demonstrate the importance of the scaffolding they provide. The deliberate teaching protocols and instructional conversations that create scaffolding actually provide multiple learning opportunities. Such opportunities promote the higher-order thinking abilities children must acquire.

Conceptually inseparable from scaffolding is a theoretical view of learning in Vygotsky's (1978) zone of proximal development (ZPD). Instruction in the ZPD is necessarily social, collaborative, affective, and cognitive. All three teachers model scaffolding features such as joint problem solving (involving children in meaningful activity and their learning by doing), intersubjectivity (coming to a shared understanding between one another, working toward a shared goal), warmth and responsiveness (creating a positive emotional tone, attributing competence to the child), and promoting self-regulation (stepping back to let children take control of their own activity, providing assistance as needed).

References

Ayers, W. 1993. *To Teach.* Portsmouth, N.H.: Heinemann.

Blathwayt, B. 1987. *Tangle and the Firesticks.* New York: Knopf.

Brown, M. 1982. *Arthur's Halloween.* Boston: Little.

Clay, M. 1985. *The Early Detection of Reading Difficulties,* 3d ed. Portsmouth, N.H.: Heinemann.

———. 1994. *Reading Recovery: A Guidebook for Teachers in Training.* Portsmouth, N.H.: Heinemann.

———. 1995. *An Observation Survey of Literacy Achievement.* Portsmouth, N.H.: Heinemann.

Clifford, E. 1979. *Help! I'm a Prisoner in the Library.* Boston: Houghton Mifflin.

Crane, S. 1976. *The Red Badge of Courage.* Secaucus, N.J.: Longriver Press.

Dahl, R. *James and the Giant Peach..* New York: Knopf.

Dewey, J. 1963. *Experience and Education.* New York: Macmillan.

Durica, K. M. 1996. *Literature Links to Phonics.* Englewood, Colo.: Teacher Ideas Press.

Edelsky, C. 1994. "Education for Democracy." *Language Arts,* 252–257.

Finchler, J. 1995. *Miss Malarkey Doesn't Live in Room 10.* New York: Walker & Co.

Fleischman, P. 1988. *Joyful Noise: Poems for Two Voices.* New York: Harper & Row.

Freire, P. 1993. *Pedagogy of the Oppressed,* 29th anniversary ed. New York: Continuum.

Gantos, Jack. 1976. *Rotten Ralph.* Boston: Houghton Mifflin.

Graves, D. 1989. *Investigating Non-Fiction.* Portsmouth N.H.: Heinemann.

Hagerty, P. 1992. *Readers' Workshop: Real Reading.* Toronto: Scholastic Canada.

Harvey, S., A. Goudris. 2000. *Strategies That Work.* York, Maine: Stenhouse.

Holdway, D. 1979. *The Foundations of Literacy.* Gosford, N.S.W.: Ashton Scholastic.

Jukes, M. 1985. *Blackberries in the Dark.* New York: Knopf.

Lipson, M., and K. Wixson. 1997. *Assessment and Instruction of Reading and Writing Disability,* 2d ed. New York: Addison-Wesley.

Lobel, Arnold. 1970. *Frog and Toad Are Friends.* New York: Harper & Row.

Minarik, E. 1957. *Little Bear.* New York: Harper & Row.

Ogle, Donna. 1986. "K-W-L: A Teaching Model that Develops Active Reading of Expository Text." *Reading Teacher,* 364–370

Parker, S. 2000. *Pond and River.* New York: Dorling and Kindersley.

Purcell-Gates, V. 1996. *Other People's Words: The Cycle of Low Literacy.* Cambridge, Mass.: HUP.

Rhodes, L., and C. Dudley-Marling. 1996. *Readers and Writers with a Difference.* Portsmouth N.H.: Heinemann.

Routman, R. 1991. *Invitations: Changing as Teachers and Learners, K–12.* Portsmouth, N.H.: Heinemann.

Schwartz, A. 1991. "In the Graveyard." In *In a Dark Room,* and other scary stories. New York: Scholastic.

Tharp, T. G. and R. Gallimore. 1995. *Rousing Minds to Life.* New York: Cambridge University Press.

Turner, A. 1986. "Read." In *Street Talk.* Dallas: Houghton Mifflin.

Vygotsky, L. 1978. *Mind in Society: The Development of Higher Psychological Processes.* Cambridge, Mass.: Harvard University Press.

Grandparents/Older People Books

Ackerman, K. 1988. *Song and Dance Man.* New York: Knopf.

Aliki. 1979. *The Two of Them.* New York: Greenwillow.

Beil, K. 1992. *Grandma According to Me.* New York: Dell.

Buting, E. 1994. *A Day's Work.* New York: Clarion.

Cazet, D. 1984. *Big Shoe, Little Shoe.* New York: Bradbury Simon & Schuster.

Cole, B. 1987. *The Trouble with Gran.* New York: Putnam.

de Paola, T. 1973. *Nana Upstairs, Nana Downstairs.* New York: Putnam.

———. 1988. *Now One Foot, Now the Other.* New York: Putnam.

———. 1993. *Tom.* New York: Putnam.

Douglas, B. 1982. *Good As New.* Fairfield N.J.: Lothrop.

Flory, J. 1977. *The Unexpected Grandchildren.* Boston: Houghton Mifflin.

Fox, M. 1984. *Wilfred Gordon McDonald Partridge.* New York: Scholastic.

Gaffney, T. 1996. *Grandpa Takes Me to the Moon.* New York: Tambourine Books.

Greenfield, E. 1988. *Grandpa's Face.* New York: Philomel.

Griffith, H. 1987. *Grandaddy's Place.* New York: Greenwillow Books.

Hest, A. 1993. *Nana's Birthday Party.* Fairfield N.J.: Morrow Junior.

Hest, A. 1984. *The Crack-of-Dawn Walkers.* New York: Macmillan.

Hest, A. 1989. *The Midnight Eaters.* New York: Four Winds Press.

Johnson, A. 1990. *When I Am Old With You.* New York: Orchard Books.

Kallier, O. 1973. *Grandma Moses.* New York: Harrison House/Abrams.

Kirk, B. 1978. *Grandpa, Me and Our House in the Tree.* New York: Macmillan.

MacLachlan, P. 1980. *Through Grandpa's Eyes.* New York: Harper & Row.

Martin, B., Jr. 1987. *Knots on a Counting Rope.* New York: Holt.

Moore, E. 1988. *Grandma's Promise.* Fairfield, N.J.: Lothrop.

Nelson, V. 1998. *Always Gramma.* New York: Putnam.

Say, A. 1993. *Grandfather's Journey.* Boston: Houghton Mifflin.

Schwartz, H. 1996. *When Artie was Little.* New York: Knopf.

Zolotow, C. 1974. *My Grandson Lew.* New York: Harper & Row.

3

The Writing Process

WITH CONTRIBUTIONS BY

DONNA WARE AND JACK GEORGE

For many teachers the surge of interest in writing process research (Graves 1983; Calkins 1994) accelerates their journeys toward personal and professional development. Such teachers attend conferences, read professional journals and books, talk with colleagues, and engage in reflective interior dialogue. Donna Ware and Jack George are no exception. And, as have most other good teachers, they learned to create classroom writing workshops according to the research *and* their own developing pedagogical knowledge. As Nancie Atwell and many others note, the teacher is central. Teachers decide, as they work with children and become better and better informed, what works in their own classrooms.

This chapter provides background on Donna's and Jack's changes and improvements. It also shows the everyday "nuts and bolts" of writing instruction in a third-grade and a fourth-grade classroom. Both writing workshops described here include extensive instruction in all the language arts, with special attention to children's literature and children's talk. We begin with Donna Ware, a third grade teacher.

Donna Ware: *Writing My Way into Becoming a Teacher of Writing*

Donna Ware is a midcareer teacher in Athens, Georgia, where the landscape and its tempo reflect a southern-living pace, especially in the summer heat. Donna has taught middle- and low-income white and diverse primary-grade students. Currently she teaches primarily middle- and low-income African American children.

56

Donna Ware

I made the decision to become a teacher at twenty-three. I was married with two babies, ages three and twelve months. My husband's job took him all over our southern state, and many times we traveled with him. In hotels with my babies I had a lot of time to think. I thought about my grandfather, who had been a teacher, and my grandmother, who encouraged me to become one. I thought about my decision not to go to college at eighteen knowing my family could not afford to send me. Then, suddenly, five years after my high school graduation, I announced that I was going to school to be a teacher. Everyone thought I was crazy, but I was determined. I made it to class by getting up at five A.M., taking my children to a sitter, and driving forty-five miles to the university. I was home by one P.M.; after putting the babies down for their afternoon naps, I studied and did housework. I knew what I wanted, and three and one-half years later, I walked into my first classroom.

My first school was a lovely, old red brick, two-level building located adjacent to the university. Many of the children were those of faculty and students, and others were children from low-income families. I struggled with primary children who ranged in reading experience from preprimer (the earliest book in first grade) to sixth grade. Then I heard about a good teacher and managed to observe her. After this observation I obtained permission from my principal to try out some of her individualized and literature-based instruction. However, I struggled with record-keeping and accountability. I had children who flourished and those who floundered. I was very frustrated.

Extending my Learning Opportunities

I decided to go back to school for my graduate degree; while there I met a professor, Dr. McNair, who changed my life forever. The first day of class he brought in a huge box of books on education. We selected what *we* wanted to read and talk about and spent the quarter doing it. Dr. McNair questioned us about what was happening in our classrooms; he challenged us to innovate and change our practices. Interestingly, his wife was the teacher I had observed the year before. The following year, I got a call from Dr. McNair, who had just become a principal in a new school. He offered me a teaching position. I accepted immediately. My new school was on the outskirts of town. We had children ranging from middle and upper-middle incomes to low incomes. My brand-new classroom had a six-foot by six-foot loft about five feet tall. Children could sit and read on the top platform and stage dramas underneath in the stage area. Dr. McNair valued the teaching of reading and writing. He arranged writing inservice sessions, encouraged teachers to attend and present at workshops, and to inspire students. We were there for one reason—to meet the needs of the children and enjoy it!

Growth and Development Interrupted

After five wonderful years Dr. McNair was transferred to another position within the district. He had helped me understand myself, accept my strengths and limitations, and do the same for my students. When Dr. McNair left, my philosophy collided with that of the new principal. I had to compromise much of what I believed. The climate of our school changed almost overnight, and teachers, accustomed to collaborating with one another and the principal, were reprimanded if they attempted to talk with him about problems. Many teachers left that year, but I did not. I felt I had a right to my school and my practice. During this difficult time I fell back on my journal writing as my therapy.

> *Journal Entry:* After lunch today I went back to my classroom to find some men tearing down my loft. I went to the principal and he said he thought it was a distraction. I asked if it could be dismantled and kept at my home. He said no. It was the property of the county. I feel as if part of *me* has been ripped out. I was told to stop my circle meetings that included lots of talk about schoolwork and feelings. I explained that these things were important for academic skills and for socialization and friendship. He said I was becoming known as the "play" teacher and he wanted to see direct instruction.

After several difficult years I transferred to another school within the district and went back to the university. That fall I began teaching third grade in a neighborhood school that supported its students and teachers. The children ranged from middle to low income and most of them walked to school, although some rode a school bus. I had taken summer graduate courses, and they were inspiring. I read Calkins, Graves, Atwell, and Routman. These authors supported my beliefs about teaching. I had been set free to teach and I plowed right in. Then, I panicked.

> *Journal Entry:* I read about the wonderful things I should be doing. It sounds so easy when I read about it. I want my class to be like those we read about. Then I get into my classroom and panic. How can I keep track of the progress of twenty-six children? I'm held accountable! I feel tied to the teacher's manual, but I also feel as if I'm being set free to "teach." But, I'm afraid of not using the supports of the basal, the spelling book, and so on. Does everything have to be covered?

That was how I experienced this period of personal and professional growth. There was considerable inner struggle as I went around and around questioning, desiring, and doubting. However, my graduate courses helped, and I began to move forward and feel less frustrated.

> *Journal Entry:* I have been in situations that did not encourage a constructivist philosophy, so I knew very little about it. But I know I've been unhappy and not teaching as well as I want to. In my eagerness to learn, I've read everything I could get my hands on. Now, I worry that I've put too much into practice too soon. I'm overwhelmed with keeping track of students' work. We just had our last graduate class meeting, and I've taken time to think about what Regie Routman (1991) says about a teacher in her book. I find I am not alone in rushing my development. ". . . [she] felt tremendous pressure to do everything, and do it well . . . was constantly looking at what others were doing . . . whenever she saw something (interesting) she wondered if she should add it to her lessons. She felt as if she should go to every workshop."

After reading this, I felt relieved. I vowed to continue to read and go about creating an environment supportive of writing.

Getting off to a Good Start

Before I began to conduct a writing workshop in my third-grade classroom, I had always loved writing with my students. We didn't write nearly as often as we needed to write—usually only one day a week. At that time, during my work with Dr. McNair, the children and I talked about writing and they wrote creative stories. I edited their writing, the children copied it over and added artwork, and I put their work up in the hall. We often spent hours on our writing and art day. It was wonderful.

That year I had a mom help me with the weekly writing days. Years later I still see this parent in the grocery store. She always mentions how much those writing days meant to her son. He was a student who struggled in school but did very well with creative applications. Our workshops connected writing to his strengths. This student and my own experiences helped fuel my desire to continue to work on writing.

I have always been concerned about teaching the many skills of writing. But one must take care not to rush the development of the workshop itself. I found it helpful to begin writers' workshop by focusing on one or two aspects of writing and having children write every day. This pace supported the children's progress and my efforts to improve my teaching. Many teachers benefit from conducting writing workshops a few days a week or with a small group in the beginning. Running a whole-class workshop is challenging. I study my teaching and avoid rushing to judgment on what seems to work and what may not. The "try everything at least five times before you decide it's not working" motto encourages patient observation. When I know what I'm trying to do is research-based and theoretically sound, I don't give up easily.

The effective writing classroom requires a high degree of structure (Graves 1983). Young writers need to learn much and they must be explicitly taught. We have to model and review a great deal in order to have a structured, productive writing community. Nancie Atwell (1998, 110–111) states:

> I need to teach my students what I expect—often again and again through the fall, until they get inside their new roles responsibilities. But first I have to figure out what my expectations are. So I think on paper about what writers and readers do, about who my students are, about what I believe and what I know, and what my priorities should be as a teacher of writing and reading.

I spend a great deal of time the first month of school teaching classroom procedures, expectations of the writing program, third grader's roles as writers, and how writers think. Minilessons at the beginning of the year are mainly procedural, as is this one.

Children receive three-ring pocket folders. I hear murmurs, "Cool, awesome. Do we get to keep them?" I feel encouraged and hopeful about this new school year. These folders include the rules and expectations of the writing workshop, paper for writing, an alphabetized section for independent spelling, and a list of the most commonly misspelled words. Also included are

Writing Log, Things I Can Do During Writing Time, Publishing Journey sheets, and a Finding Focus Web. (See the Appendix.) Each of these items is a focus of future minilessons.

I expect students to write every day. If they write on a daily basis they write more, acquire a disposition for writing, and see themselves as writers. If I require daily writing I must support it. Writing topics become critical. On the first day of school I model creating a topic list. I begin by reading a piece of literature such as Baylor's (1995) *I'm in Charge of Celebrations* or Ryland's (1985) *When I Was Young in the Mountains.*

- After a brief discussion of the book, I tell the students that they will spend a lot of time writing this year. Writers such as Baylor or Rylant write about things they know, love, and feel strongly about. Writers keep lists of things they might like to write about. I tell students that today as writers we are going to begin a topic list.

- Using the overhead I begin to list things I might write about. I draw the children into the conversation as I jot down topics, such as books I like, places I've visited, and the techniques of riding a mountain bike (one of my passions). I show how a topic list grows and changes.

I continue in this way, listening to the children and talking with them. I see several children pulling out paper and beginning their own lists. Breanna and Tessa ask if they can write about their pets. Cody wants to know if he can write about football and his cousin. Sam and Fisher have new go-carts and want to tell us about them. Sharing is an important aspect of a writing classroom (often with as much or more talk than writing). This builds a sense of belonging in a writing community and better writing. I have students discuss their writing ideas and give them about five minutes to work on their lists independently. They then work in small groups or with a partner to talk more and extend their lists. This lesson provides the opportunity to recycle the idea of topic lists, scaffolds actual list writing, and fosters collaboration.

Good writers are constantly aware of their surroundings, looking for writing topics, jotting ideas down in their journals or on a napkin, and so on. We practice by looking outside, around the room and school, taking note of possible topics. To ensure that students have a constant supply of ideas, we revisit their topic lists often throughout the school year.

When reading literature I encourage students to make connections to their own lives with questions such as, Have you ever felt this way? Has this ever happened to you? Why do you suppose the author wrote about this? This topic is important to this author; do you feel the same?

These questions provide support for learning about how writers think, and this thinking works into children's writing. When students listen to their peers share their writing, they often piggyback ideas from one another.

I administer writing interviews that generate more writing and topics. I model and review constantly to structure a productive writing community. In the beginning my minilessons are mainly procedural. For example they are on topics such as

- general workshop routines, coming to group meetings, and what happens during writing and conference times
- how writing folders are dealt with, how to hold a peer conference, what to do when you need help, and how to use the publishing journey sheet

Once the students have a good understanding of their roles as writers and the procedures of the writing class, I can begin to help them discover the words and the tools they will need to react to and interact with their world. I do this through minilessons that focus on an opportunity to teach explicitly the skills and strategies needed. The following schedule works for me. The writing workshop usually lasts from forty to sixty minutes on this schedule:

- interactive listening and talking while sharing of a poem, a chapter or picture book, or pieces of nonfiction writing
- a minilesson that covers writing conventions, use of vivid language, leads, or workshop procedures
- status of the class—a quick check to see what each child is working on
- quiet writing time, in which students write and I work my way around the room to talk to individual children
- conference time

The class comes together to discuss how things went for the day and to share work in progress or completed pieces. This conclusion of the workshop takes additional time. I'd like more time but the school schedule does not make this possible.

The interactive listening and talking time helps all of us warm up. We discuss authors' purpose, choice of character, setting, and other features of literature appropriate to what is being shared and discussed. I often comment on the authors' use of strong language and verbs—how the author shows rather than tells. Children make notes in their writer's notebooks. Notebooks become powerful resources of recorded thoughts, words, and ideas.

The status-of-the-class record (Atwell 1998, 140–142) is an effective tool for keeping track of students' writing. This record check each day helps the children commit to the self-selected writing tasks. However, some assigned writings are done for teaching genre and other things such as how books work and author's purpose. Quiet writing time is pretty obvious. This is when the children actually write, and it provides time for me to identify needs and make quick teaching points on spelling, use of details, leads, and so on. Most teaching points take only moments and are much more effective than lectures. Conference time is used to reemphasize skills, procedures, and writing lessons such as topic focus, character development, and finding one's voice.

Throughout the conference period, I consider ideas for a whole-group "quick teach." At the end of conference time, when the class gets together for sharing, I can teach again. These minilessons are enriched because they come directly from the growth and struggles the children have just experienced.

Organization of materials is important in every writing workshop. Here are ways I've found to handle materials effectively:

- Writing notebooks hold manuscripts; writing notebooks go in plastic crates.
- Baskets hold book covers, colored pens, markers, thesaurus, and spelling dictionaries.
- Stacked bins hold student writing based on the publishing journey (first, second, and third drafts, etc.).
- Written organizers and posters are on the walls around the room to help the classroom run smoothly.

Moving Toward a Better Writing Workshop

The writing workshop just described was well organized and supported the students and me. But, the quality of the children's writing didn't seem to be improving. They wrote daily, shared writing, and read good literature—but they were not connecting skills or integrating them well enough. When I typed the children's stories, I noticed many things we could have worked on to improve their writing. I went back to school and did some soul-searching about my writing program. I came across a book by JoBeth Allen and Jana Mason (1992, 27) called *Risk Makers; Risk Takers; Risk Breakers.* These authors helped me a great deal when they wrote:

> The notion of placing children in the center of evaluation is new to most of us. For decades, we have been the ones who decided whether students were doing well, and we thought it was our responsibility to motivate children. [Thus,] they come to rely on us too much, and learned helplessness may set

in . . . the task is how to move the initiative from our court into theirs . . . they must be able to show proof that they are making progress, and they must decide what they want to read or write. They must know when to ask for help and must have help readily available to them. Our policy is to support independent learners.

After reading this book, I concluded that the children's self-assessment was missing from my writing program. I expected my students to be motivated by my lessons, and sometimes they were and sometimes they weren't. I found that the quality of my students' writing did not improve unless they self-assessed their own work and set their own goals. Students are much more motivated and the quality of their writing increases when they self-assess. Here are some examples of one student's self-assessment comments.

Sam: My stories are more realistic and, at the beginning of the year I wouldn't put people talking [in] very much and, they'd just be really short like a paragraph or something and they wouldn't be very exciting or anything. My goal is to publish more stories I write because most of the time I write stories and then I start a new one and I see I've only published two stories.

Sam's notebook was stuffed with pieces. He realized in self-assessing that he had written a great deal but not carried it through.

Finally, improvements in my program have come about because I have high—but reasonable—expectations about writing that help decrease pressure. Not every child writes well every single day. (What writer can?) On an off day, a child can try to write, albeit briefly, be a good listener, and read more. Sometimes a sentence or two is all a writer of any age can manage. This kind of flexibility helps reduce the likelihood that the writing workshop routines become a grind. Teachers depend on routines to help sustain everyday classroom experiences. But, in doing so we must take care not to get into a rut. The writing process does dry up from time to time, and writers, young and old, need refreshing breaks and a change of pace.

Revising is very difficult for young writers (as well as older ones!). It's very hard work. In addition, what my third-graders write is "a part of them." Even when peers ask questions about confusing parts of their stories and give suggestions, many children balk at going back and changing their writing. The development of the writer's disposition to revise takes time. I do not push revision at the beginning of the year. I address the topic of revision more toward the middle and end of the year through minilessons and by showing writings of other children.

Small Lessons with Big Results: Using Graphic Organizers and Extended Lessons to Improve Writing

An addition to my expanding efforts to learn to teach writing is the use of graphic organizers. (See the Appendix for an example, and try other culturally significant days—move beyond U.S. and European family celebrated occasions.) When my students choose topics to write about, they invariably choose very broad topics, such as a pet, playing baseball, or a vacation. To help them focus I use a double web. Here is an example:

Day 1

- Ask the children to share their favorite ride at a theme park. (Write and circle theme park on chart paper and then add the children's ideas all around it, forming the first web).
- Read *The Screaming Mean Machine* (Cowley 1993). Discuss how the author chose one ride to write about.
- Revisit the first web and choose a ride as an example. Brainstorm with the children about the features of this ride.

Day 2:

- Put a blank web on the overhead, give the children copies of the overhead, and select a topic such as "my best friend." Decide on a focus, such as "things we do together" and have each child fill out this web as you fill out yours on the overhead.
- Put up another blank web and give out copies of it. Pull a topic from the first web, such as "spend the night together," and brainstorm ideas about this more focused topic. Complete as before.

Day 3:

- Bring binoculars to class and talk about how they help people see distant objects more clearly. Read two pieces of writing, one with a tight focus and another that takes on a broad topic. Ask the children which was more focused. Give them writing samples and have them "use their writer's binoculars" to locate more focused topics. Discuss these ideas at length.

Day 4:

- Have children use a double web to plan a focused piece of writing of their choice. Invite sharing.

Using the double-web set of lessons has helped my students tremendously, as has the following lesson on helping students become aware of strong verbs. Here is an outline of how it goes.

Day 1:

- Show a poem with strong verbs on overhead. Read it to the class, prompt children to work through it, identifying action words, circle these words, and discuss how they help make the poem more exciting.

Day 2:

- Repeat the process (with the child's permission, a writing sample can be used instead of a poem).

Day 3:

- Have the children choose a piece of writing, locate the verbs, and circle them. Let them decide if the verbs are exciting enough and use a thesaurus to edit.

Day 4:

- Invite the children to experiment using strong verbs in their quiet writing time. Invite sharing (this technique works well with adjectives, pronouns, and so on).

Spelling: At the Core of Writing Workshop

Research reminds us of what teachers need to know, namely, that learning to spell is a complex process. Children do not learn to spell with equal ease or in the same way. Spelling may seem natural for some children, but others may find it extremely difficult.

In every writers' workshop, spelling must be taught well. Based on the work of Gentry and Gillet (1993) and Wilde (1992), I built a spelling program that supports children's independent learning. Children use various supports, such as the word wall (described later), asking a peer, trying to spell a word on their own before asking the teacher, and using the dictionary. Children come to me for help. I coach with various prompts and explicit teaching such as, "You have all the letters correct but they are in the wrong order. Try again." After saying this I place a check mark above the letters the child has correct and rewrite the word, leaving blanks for the missing letters.

Often children need to talk about spelling and its role in writing. Classroom discussion builds awareness, stronger strategies, and independence, as this conversation with DeMont shows.

Teacher: DeMont, what makes a good writer?

D: If he can spell good.

Teacher: What if someone doesn't know how to spell a word. What can he do?

D: Ask a friend. When I need a word I always go ask a friend.

Teacher: What else can you do with a spelling problem?

D: Well, I try to spell it the best way I can and when I get my Have-a-Go sheet, I try to spell it again, see what part I have right. Then if I still can't get it, I go get the dictionary.

The children learn that I am not going to give them the answer. I let them know that they need to be more self-reliant. With a secure structure about what to do if they can't spell a word, adequate time, and the clear message that I expect them to work responsibly, children more readily become independent.

Other actions support spelling instruction in the primary classroom. I have posted lists of high-frequency sight words on the classroom walls. Don Holdaway (1979) calls these words the *bedrock* of sight vocabulary. I arrange the words in alphabetical order, *A* words on one colored sheet of paper, *B* words on another color, and so on.

Children learn to use wall lists, or word walls, and I guide them to the pattern and color they need if they can't find it. Another technique to use is word rhymes. Teremekia was stuck on the word *ground.* This word was not on the word wall, so I asked her to come up with a rhyming word. She named *sound* which was on the word wall. I asked her to look again at the blue S words and find the word *sound.* She immediately located it and said, "Oh, now I know how to spell it, g-r-o-u-n-d."

Children see words on the word wall daily, and they use them to get their writing done. Both my teaching and children's "word use" are critical in their learning to spell. Notice in the following example how spelling gets done in our workshop.

Many children in the room are in the editing process. Sammie Ann, Tabitha, and Chris are huddled together reading each other's stories. Jared and Carl have red pens and are busy searching for words that "don't look right." DeMont has his Have-a-Go sheet with a list of five misspelled words. He has corrected the first three on his own but comes to me for help on the last two. He is working on *families* and has written *fmlys.* I praise the work he has done correctly.

- "Good, let's look at what is right about this word!" Then, I write it out his way and leave blanks for missing letters (f_m_l_ _s).
- DeMont's second attempt results in *famalies*. I ask how he knew to add *i-e-s*.
- DeMont says, "I remembered needing to change *y* to *i*."
- I give him the letter *i* (instead of *a*) and again congratulate him for working hard and getting so much right.
- Finally, I remind DeMont to put *families* in his personal dictionary.

As use of the word wall grows, I add math, science, and social studies words we need. Again and again, if I truly watch the children at work, I learn how to teach better.

Conclusion

I sit back and watch the children as they dance their way through writing workshop day after day. I move from desk to desk asking "How is it going? Will you share what you wrote with me? What are your plans for this?" I gather a group of students, Danny, Simon, and Mark around me for a conference. Other children form small groups of their own for peer conferences. Angela, a child in my group shares a piece of writing and I begin to ask "What questions do you have for her? What do you like about Helen's piece? Were there any parts of Harry's writing that weren't clear to you?" We finish and I move around the room to check on other groups. I am excited to hear the children asking each other similar questions about their writing. The program is running smoothly. I know it will take continued effort and change to sustain and improve it, but I enjoy this moment.

I want to conclude with two poems. The first poem expresses the role writing has in my personal life and in my teaching.

> How can I flatten life onto a piece of paper?
> How can I take a life that is round and full
> and flatten it onto a piece of paper.
> I need words.
> The words are in children's voices,
> words to make life round and full.
>
> D. Ware

This second poem reveals some of the satisfaction I continue to gain from my life as a classroom teacher. Neither poem is meant to obscure the struggles I've had nor those to come, for teaching effectively is always a challenge.

> The room is bare,
> the shelves covered,
> the desks emptied and pushed to the center of the room.
> Another year boxed up and stored away
> but the voices of my students echo off the walls and
> there are visions of them
> clustered together
> heads together
> talking, writing, editing.
> Visions of students creating.
>
> *D. Ware*

For the Instructional Conversation

In-Class or In-Group Thinking, Writing, and Talking

1. For the next week, keep a daily journal. If you are teaching, write about that. If you are not teaching, write about something else that you are trying to do (going to school, parenting, learning something new). This may be done in or outside of class or group meetings. Share an entry or two from your journal with a small group on a regular basis. Discuss the insights gained from keeping a journal.

2. Reread Donna's discussion in Chapter 1 about feeling controlled at school and wondering whether children feel similarly when they are controlled. Respond to this passage with a five-minute quick write and discuss your writing with someone nearby. In addition to your own immediate response, focus on questions such as, "What does it mean to be controlled?" and "How does control influence learning?" Share insights, different perceptions, and questions within the large group.

3. Reread the questions about professional development at the beginning of Chapter 1. Apply these questions to Donna and her practice. Jot down your response(s) to each question and discuss them with two or three other people. Collaborate to combine your lists and refine your ideas. Discuss your ideas with others and see how they agree or disagree.

Reflective Thinking and Action

1. Take three to five class or meeting periods and conduct a writing work-shop following some of Donna's description of her program as it is to-day. Be sure all participants publish a text in some way (even if just to share aloud). As a class, outline the strategies that were implemented, and discuss these strategies.

   To extend the second activity in the In-Class section, use two or more additional readings on controlling/empowering teachers and write a short paper on the principal's efforts to control Donna's teach-ing. Essentially, Donna was told to stop doing what she believed was best for children. Respond to these questions in your writing: What roles should administrators have in situations of this nature? How much autonomy should teachers have? Should empowerment extend to teachers as we expect it to be extended to children? What kind of teacher prefers control? Why do you think a teacher would have this preference?

2. With a partner prepare a presentation for your peers on Donna's view of teacher responsibility. Donna believed she was responsible for how much students learn. To what extent and in what ways are teachers responsible? To what extend and in what ways are teachers not (completely—or at all) responsible?

3. Select two books that Donna says were important in her practice. Or select two other books on teaching writing. Read these books for the purpose of comparing and contrasting their similarities in structuring a writing or a reading and writing workshop and for their philoso-phies. Make notes as you read and develop a poster presentation or a playlet that portrays the kind of workshop you would like to have in your classroom (in a playlet you act out your role and that of a student in a ten- to fifteen-minute dramatization).

Jack George: Poetry and the Language Arts for Engaging Learners

Jack George is a New Yorker. He teaches racially diverse, low-income children. The northeastern lifestyle of Jack and his students contrasts with the southern liv-ing pace of Donna and her students. Yet his and her students' strengths and needs are very similar. Also similar are Jack's and Donna's personal and professional experiences with writing and their understanding of what writing does for the growth and development of teachers and children.

Jack George

There was a time when I thought all journeys had a beginning and an end and in between there were events that made up that experience. I was naive enough to think that my teaching and learning would follow that course. Not until I became philosophically grounded with constructivist learning theory did I realize that the career I had chosen would never really come to a journey's end, at least not in the traditional sense of reaching a point where I could say, "I have arrived."

How it Was Then

I started my journey many years ago in a sixth-grade classroom in school E 360 at a time when the basals dictated the direction and content of the curriculum. Unfortunately, I'm not sure that the situation has changed in most classrooms. I used basals, spewed the questions, and listened as the kids regurgitated the answers. I waited, often impatiently, because the only acceptable answers were those that had been generated by experts who "knew" children and had spent many years studying and developing appropriate questions and answers, or so I was informed at the time. The parameters of learning were rather narrow. I conformed to the limits dictated by an inner-city system that primarily served low-income children from diverse cultures. As the teacher I experienced no flexibility and, to my everlasting sorrow, neither did my students.

Within a few months after I became a teacher, my fatherlike principal congratulated me for doing a first-rate job. He spent a good deal of time telling me that I had an orderly classroom of quiet children who used good manners and were not disruptive. As they say, the "blinds were straight." The students and I even ate lunch in relative quiet. The school imperative was: Children listen to your teacher and wait to be called on.

It didn't take very long for me to become annoyed with the mass of grading boring worksheets and spelling tests. In our assigned texts, no pages were to be skipped or amended. We were checked on to be sure that we followed the sequence of the scripts written by experts. I questioned the expertise of these authors, but at the time I had neither the experience nor the moxy to challenge them.

I sensed the need for change—I knew this way of teaching did not do justice to my students. But I also knew I was a part of a huge entity, namely, the school district that ground away at its methodical pace. It took me longer to realize that the way I was teaching also did not do justice to me. I wasn't learning anything! I lived in a world (as some still do) in which a curriculum director checked my page number in reading and math to be sure I was on the right page at the right time of year. The workbooks, teachers' manuals, and standardized tests drove me crazy as they drove my teaching.

In addition, the tons of grades I gave communicated little if any meaning to the children or me. I was too busy assigning grades and keeping records. I didn't have time to truly know the child I was grading. As I consider the time and energy it took to apply this curriculum and assessment system, I see how it dictated and limited my and my students' intellectual lives. The schedule ruled. There was no way to adjust or work around special subjects and certainly no time for thinking. My reading lessons were so carefully planned that I could split that sixty-minute block into three perfectly timed twenty-minute segments. Group I (Bluebirds) would be in flight with me while group II (Hawks) fluttered hopelessly in the workbook and group III (Robins) pecked away at the (additional!) backup worksheets. The Robins followed with a worksheet check as the Hawks started on the next story. I have no idea how I maintained my sanity. I even caught myself falling asleep when oral reading was in full swing. It happened when the Robins (the *low* group) chirped away at uninspiring texts. My head nodded, I caught myself, and then glanced to see if I'd been discovered.

The Power of the Need for Change

I felt less and less content—that pebble in my shoe grew to boulder size. I decided to make some changes within the limits to which I could stretch. I began teaching science outdoors whenever the weather permitted. In our urban environment there was a vacant lot not too far away, so it worked out. The children loved it and their learning improved. I began to incorporate drama, and the children wrote plays and performed puppet shows. The children loved their drama work even more. I could see the growth in all of us. Drama was a beginning of teaching and learning on a new level; it included all the language arts, problem solving, purpose, collaboration, community building (so necessary for my students and me), creativity, and math (we constructed a stage as well as puppets). I couldn't have articulated it at the time, but now I know that drama projects made so much sense to the children. In drama, written language is extremely meaningful—it so clearly creates meaning. As the children's engagement increased, I realized that their interest was of utmost importance for their learning. Still, with good things happening before my eyes, I made some mistakes, such as having the children working on a topic *I* selected. I did not yet have the theory base I needed to move more quickly toward instructional improvement.

A New Beginning

One summer my journey quickened. I applied for and got a new teaching position that led to teaching fourth grade. I had heard about the principal, Ms. Lynch, who had the reputation of being very progressive. In spite of warnings from my colleagues—"You won't like it"—I wanted to find another way of living my teaching life. Early on I was observed by Ms. Lynch. I was nested with my (new) Robins and teaching with the basal. I persisted with my lesson and was delighted to discover that Ms. Lynch was primarily interested in how I dealt with the children and the kind of atmosphere I created for learning. Ms. Lynch and I had many conversations about children's ownership, self-selection, using children's literature in teaching, and writing and its power to transform. I was transformed by this dialogue and by the stance Ms. Lynch had toward me, the other teachers, and especially the children. I felt empowered and took seriously this principal's advice to "take risks and if it didn't work to think about what went wrong and learn from it." She gave us license to try—and I did. I read articles and research reports in *Reading Teacher, Language Arts,* and *Educational Leadership.*

I hadn't read many educational journals over the years because my teaching context didn't call for it. After all, if the answers were in the books I had to use then, and as long as I went by the book there was no need for me to think for myself.

I was eager but I was hard pressed in this new context to keep up with the readings in which the whole staff engaged. Here I was after many years of teaching being "the new kid on the block." I learned much about the constructivist approach and literature-based teaching from younger colleagues and Ms. Lynch.

In a short year's time, I experienced a revelation. I realized I had found freedom! Not freedom to do anything, but freedom to engage in a wholly accountable trek toward learning to teach. Here is an early event that took place in the new school to which I belonged.

I began work on journals and engaged in the most authentic teaching I'd ever done. I was smitten by my mentors, Jerry Harste, Dorothy Watson, the Goodmans, Donald Graves, Nancie Atwell, Judith Newman, Reggie Routman, and many others. When the fall term came around the next year I greeted my new class of fourth graders with a nervous smile and a "New Year's Party," complete with balloons, cookies, and a day set aside for learning about one another. That year I began to teach reading with literature (and no basal).

In the Trenches

I was used to feeling confident and experienced. Now I felt unsure and wondered if risk-taking was all it was cracked up to be. I stretched out the morning of the second day of school as long as possible. I probably set a new record for the longest pledge to the flag! I felt my armpits getting warm, looked at my nine- and ten-year-olds and began. "Good morning girls and boys, let's start with a 1979 poem by Shel Silverstein" (a classic children's poet who remains a favorite).

Well, nobody responded, not a cheer, not a boo, not a word. I felt terrible. I persisted with Silverstein's "Invitation." Then we talked about being welcomed into a learning community; we talked about belonging there. That went well. However, later that day and in days to come I was tempted to use the basals that were still on my shelf. I still needed that "for sure" support. Somehow I knew that I was not going to move backward, so I steered away from them. This move was necessary for my personal and professional development at this time, though now I know how to use quality-literature basals in effective ways without being dependent on them.

It was there in school C112 with more than four hundred low-income children with abounding social problems that I truly learned to teach. Parents looked to the school and me for a safe and accepting environment. We worked hard to meet the needs of the community and of every child. A constructivist philosophy was key to our success.

Poetry: Its Frustrations and Its Glories

In this section I focus on some whole-class poetry instruction and how I've worked with poetry and reluctant learners. Poetry, a genre that is often avoided by even experienced adults, has become the cornerstone of my writing program. I believe that this is so because of my own experiences in learning to write poetry as an adult. I know what it's like to write poetry and how to appreciate it as a reader. Thus, I have a strength that I use very deliberately in my teaching.

Children would benefit if more teachers valued their own interests enough to incorporate them into their instruction. Nearly any personal hobby or vocation of the teacher can become an excellent instructional resource. Bringing ourselves into the curriculum enriches our lives as teachers. When teachers are happier in the classroom, they are much better teachers. We owe it to our students as much as to ourselves to be happier in the classroom.

Poetry Instruction

My fourth graders find Shel Silverstein, Jack Prelutsky, Jeff Moss, Eloise Greenfield, and Judith Viorst to be among their favorite poets. And I find that poetry affords ways to teach many language conventions and skills. It is the way it affords opportunities to play with language, however, that is important to my reluctant learners. All too often students do not experience language play in the early grades or at home. So I've made it my business to invent some concrete ways of teaching it. I've found that learning to play with language is essential in learning to write.

At the beginning of the year I issue a poetic license to each child. This simple formality gives many children the freedom they need to risk trying to write and read poetry without fear of making a mistake.

_____has been given his/her
Poetic License for the school year_____.
This license entitles you to take risks in your writing by trying new words, making up new forms for old words, and making up fun words that will help you express yourself when writing poems and stories. As a writer, you will be allowed to bend some rules and find interesting new ways to communicate. You have my permission to use your license in class whenever you wish.

Jack George
Director of Licensing

The Poetic License is clear and concrete. Children tape it to their desks. To demonstrate poetic license and to model the role of word and language play, I begin with a poem by Odgen Nash (1997):

The Octopus

Tell me, oh Octopus, I begs
Is those things arms, or is they legs?
I marvel at thee, Octopus;
If I were thou, I'd call me Us.

After reading the poem from an overhead projector (children must see poetic language as well as hear it), the lesson goes something like this.

- I ask, "What did this poet do?"
- The children respond in various ways, such as, "How can he say, 'Tell me, oh Octopus, I begs, is those things arms, or is they legs'?"
- Or they ask critical questions, such as, "That's not the way to write, is it?"
- I talk about the poet's use of poetic license to make the poem work.

The influence of this kind of instruction is illustrated through a bright student who hardly ever worked up to her ability. In working with poetry, she came up with a good beginning alliteration and nonsense poem (fourth graders are really into nonsense).

Wiggly, waggly, woggly, Willie washed his wig.

As useful as poetic licenses are in getting children started, I move on to other poetry fairly soon, keeping the poetic license in play. More serious topics help show what poetry does. Namely, it invites participation in the experience. It also opens the teacher's door to instruction on literary elements. Character, setting, theme, and more elements are in poetry just waiting to be taught.

- After showing the children a poem on the overhead, I point out elements such as point of view, character, etc.
- I give students sheets with poetry elements and brief definitions or examples. And I show them another poem.
- This time the class then helps me identify and discuss the poetry elements in the new poem.

As noted previously, I focus on teaching children how to actually write poetry as well as how to critically analyze it. To teach poetry writing, we begin, as usual, with a class discussion. My part of the conversation is loosely organized around the following goals:

- Introduce the concept (in this case, poems with serious topics).
- Watch for what children already know, because this is the real starting point.
- Help the class brainstorm to pull ideas together. This primes an individual writer's thinking.

- List the ideas on the overhead or board and set limits so children can write in safety (write nothing that would embarrass you, your family, or your class).

I like a wide range of freedom for my students. And I rarely have to curb a child's interest in a topic. Children have to write about what is real and salient to them. Here are some examples of ideas my fourth graders come up with:

My dog died, my best friend move, my aunt lost her job, I have lots of homework, I failed in math, my mom grounded me, I hate going to church, and my bike broke.

I tell children to take an idea from our brainstorming or another of their own and write a sentence or two about it. Here is what another student created:

I felt sad when my dog Jake died of old age.
He was a big hound dog who loved to howl.
He won't ever again.

With this child's permission I put her words on the overhead and suggested that the class work on taking out all but words that were essential to her meaning. This helps children see that poems distill language and how free verse (without rhyming) functions, and it easily teaches a strategy for writing poetry.

After some trial and error and much discussion, the class wrote a first draft that read, "Jake died. Old age. Our hound won't howl again." This produced a good lesson and rendered a pleasing draft with which our young author could work.

Things don't always go smoothly. Teaching children about the efficiency of words and importance of word choice in writing poetry can be challenging. I find guiding them through the process as a group helps them learn most efficiently. Later on children can do this same kind of work in small groups and on their own. It's nice when my own teaching experiences are in agreement with expert researchers such as Vygotsky (1978), who held that what children can do today in cooperation they can do independently tomorrow. Another Vygotsky (1978, 22–23) point is also important in my growth and development. "A child's speech is as important as the role of action in attaining the goal. If children are not allowed to use speech, they cannot accomplish the task. Children solve practical tasks with the help of their speech, as well as their eyes and hands." This quote led me to understand the importance of supporting conversation in my class. Children's talk became a critical part of learning and the hum of the classroom became music (before it was noise). My poetic energy was reinforced by Vygotsky's vision because oral poetry and conversation about poems became the vehicles with which many children gained a voice in the classroom.

About the same time that the class was producing poems on the dog Jake, our resident sports fan also wrote. This child was a hockey player who disliked math but was interested in writing. His first effort produced some nice lines that could stand alone or be worked with for later publication.

> The puck flew past a dot,
> Into the net, we won.

Later that week, out one of my female students began a persuasive essay with this poem,

> Desks are cool, don't be a fool. Tables are neat, with
> room for feet.

This poem came out of a class discussion on working together and the ways that tables, rather than desks in rows, help people collaborate. The talk about working together was part of a larger discussion about how much it helps individual writers to be in a classroom community in which everyone is thinking, talking about, and doing poetry.

Yet there were troubling times for me as a person and as a teacher. The inconsistency of children's writing frustrated and worried me. However, in reading authors such as Donald Graves, I learned an important lesson. The "inconsistencies" I saw were part of the writing and learning process. As Graves (1983, 270) notes, "Writing is a highly idiosyncratic process that varies from day to day. Variance is the norm, not the exception." This insight led me to be more accepting and improved my instruction; now I could help the children understand that variance in writing from day to day was okay as long as they persisted in writing and tried out my suggestions for improvement. For some children (and for me) this was a tremendous relief and freed them to continue to write in spite of difficulties. One more thing Donald Graves said at a conference presentation helped me a great deal. On giving advice to teachers of writing, he said, "Shut up, listen, and learn." What amazing advice for any teacher, especially those of us who at one time thought we were (or should be) the center of the classroom. This and other advice from the literature helped me greatly as I continued to make my journey toward learning to teach.

As I indicated previously, I work with children who have not written much in school. They are struggling literacy learners. Here are some classroom examples of just such children.

Reaching Reluctant Learners

Thad and James were members of my first fourth-grade class. Both boys were weighed down educationally and emotionally. The boys lived up to their tough-guy images. I worried about them. Neither youngster seemed disposed to invest in learning.

In that year, I plunged into modeling oral reading every day with books such as *Hugh Glass Mountain Man* by McClung (1990) and other books with exciting themes and plenty of action. I often "got dramatic," standing on chairs and using voice changes to spark interest. Most of the children loved it, but I couldn't reach Thad and James. Then one day I tried some other kinds of poems and selected Shel Silverstein to generate more interest. I read an animated version of "The Googies are Coming." This poem contains a lively, tongue-in-cheek verse about googies coming to buy little children. That line caught both boys' attention, and as I finished enacting the poem the most proactive child volunteered, "I like that Mr. George." In that stunning moment I thought, "Wow!"

We reread and spent time with this poem as we did math and wrote word problems (the poem lends itself to that). We worked hard and the boys engaged, discovering that learning is both fun and work.

Thad wasn't exactly hooked on poetry, but the bait had tempted him. It took much more teaching to support his genuine caring. James had participated to an extent I'd never seen before and I was hopeful about the lure of poetry for him. What I didn't know at the time was that I wouldn't have had to work nearly as hard if I'd offered more self-selection to all the children and especially to reluctant readers and writers. I've learned since that I need to select a pool of poetry and present it in attractive and challenging ways and then let the children dive in. They need to read what is most interesting to them (not me). At that time I controlled what was read. I needed to structure instruction better and then support more student decision making.

The Power of Ownership

One of the most reluctant writers with whom I've ever worked was Brian. He hated to write. Even in fourth grade, producing one line was nearly impossible—and he went to great lengths to avoid trying at all. I had to move very slowly and carefully with him.

The reading specialists and I worked together with Brian; we took very small steps that felt safe to him. He chose to read easy poems that he could practice and present to the class. This provided less risk for him and an opportunity to experience success. Essentially, Brian was building his own confidence in this self-selected activity. It was exactly what needed to happen.

I tried to be ready for any moment that would give him an opportunity to risk producing his own writing. One day in a writing conference I told Brian I had a bad morning. I told him I had to put my dog to sleep and that it made me very sad. He looked at me in a way I'd not seen before. Later that day Brian actually put down words on paper and came to me to see if I wanted to look at his writing. I was glad to do so (he had no idea how glad). Brian showed me his poem about his father, who had passed away years before. I struggled to do justice to the poem as I read it aloud.

> Dad is in the sky
> if you can know
> you can hear me
> please come and fly by.

Poetry had touched the heart of this little boy. This was a powerful effort from a child who hated to write. I thought then that he had never before written something that was truly for himself. All children must write for themselves—in their own voices. To do this they need a audience (teachers and peers are so important). They need their own reasons to write. Thus, a true purpose helps sustain the considerable effort that writing demands. In my teaching, a poetry focus has helped students find their purposes for writing.

With Brian's permission, we used his poem to show editing and revision on the class overhead. He was thrilled by the attention. Brian left me this note.

Dear Mr. George

Thank you for making a sample of me in reading today.
I am happy.

Brian

Later we got his poem published in the school newspaper and a struggling student had his moment in the sun. Publication is essential for all students. It takes place easily in the classroom. It can be expanded by school and grade-level newspapers and by special presentations in the principal's office, in other classrooms, the lunchroom, and so on. Toward the end of the school year Brian wrote again spontaneously to both the reading specialist and me.

Dear Teachers,

Thank you for helping me be a better writer this year, and I like to read a lot more too.

Brian

Moments such as these are the lifeblood of teaching. I was so proud of him. As he finished fourth grade, we spent more time on writing conventions and continued to model good writing. Supporting Brian could be tedious and it was slow. But we made progress! I still grin when I think of what Brian gave us. Interestingly, Brian continues to give to me. In a recent contact with Brian's mother, she let me know that he was doing well in school! His mom asked that his name be used in this book. She and Brian are very proud of his writing—and justly so.

Poetry Works at Any Age

In addition to fourth-graders, I've reached younger children with poetry. The next example comes from a summer-school class in which I had two special students.

First-graders Henry and Wilson were foster brothers, and both had serious reading and writing problems. Both children came from alcohol- and drug-addicted parents. Henry was cooperative once he trusted me, but that took a long time. Wilson was always on guard and unwilling to take risks. With so little experience with written language, this meant he literally refused to read or write. The boys were a challenge. My task was to get them to invest in print in some meaningful way.

After a week of their resistance, I resorted to my ace in the hole. I used poems by Marc Brown (1985) entitled *Hand Rhymes.* I had most of the verses on chart paper hanging around the room. Here is an approximation of how this literacy event went.

First: I read and enacted the poems and I asked the children to join me.

Second: Boy 1 sneered, "That's stupid," and put his head down on his desk.

Third: Boy 2 replied, "I'll do it, Mr. George," looking at his foster brother with a big grin.

Fourth: The class joined boy 2, and after a bit of review, I turned over the poem presentations to them alone.

Fifth: Boy 1 raised his hand and joined in a small, listless effort. (But he joined in!)

This breakthrough was enough to make me smile and consider the power of the social interactions that were taking place. I pursued working with the Marc Brown poetry for several days, supporting the children in polishing their reading and enactments.

Children love to perform when they have sufficient support and a no-pressure environment. My students perform only after they have asked to do so. As we worked with poetry, I took advantage of opportunities to explicitly teach phonics, such as pointing out letter and sound relationships once the children were really interested in poetry. As we worked, boy 2 unexpectedly asked if we could do the poems for his sister's class.

Of course we did. With an authentic reason to read and lots of practice, their poetry performance was terrific. There is nothing like an audience to improve the language arts! (How could I have overlooked this?) I was so proud that students felt that they could ask for things and voice their opinions. My class avidly engaged with print, and they did so while grinning from ear to ear. The importance of their enjoyment cannot be overstated. And audience, authenticity, teacher support, and collaborative opportunities made the risk of learning worth taking. For my two very reluctant learners, these factors were key. Another key was the immersion of my students in poetry. I had a gut feeling that children needed to be surrounded with poetry, but reading Carol Avery (1985, 292–293) confirmed it. She notes,

> When I read lots of poetry and invite children to respond to the rhythm, sound, and images that poetry invokes, children begin writing poetry. I've never been comfortable with formulas for writing poetry that I've seen in some language arts books. The children in my classroom follow the model of the poems themselves and only a small portion of their finished poems rhyme.

This idea led me to creating more open and inviting classrooms, where enjoying poetry became a daily event.

The Power of Drama

In addition to poetry, drama steers a straight course into children's hearts and minds. Drama includes all sorts of problem solving, sharing, community building, creative, and a number of skills from various areas of study. Here are some specific examples of what drama can do.

- It helps keep written language very meaningful.

- In playacting, words are used to create physical meaning.

- The physical elements in drama hold children's interest like none other.

I began to use drama in the classroom very simply with puppet shows and later progressed to fully staged presentations.

Drama projects gave many children a way to contribute. Beyond doing a great deal of writing, they found nontraditional ways to participate, such as prompting and practicing lines with one another, working on staging, and so on. In doing so, they found a way to belong; so much of becoming a learner involves a "sense of belonging." This is true of teachers, too.

The following story of a boy I'll call Roy is a good case in point. Roy was a round-shouldered ten-year-old with bright blue eyes and a swaggering walk. Yet as tough as Roy tried to act, he pulled back in most learning situations like a turtle in hiding. Roy was in the principal's office regularly for inappropriate behavior, fighting, and—most frequently—for using bad language. I knew he needed help. I also knew that no one was at home in the late afternoon, so one day I asked him to stay after school to help build the stage. Building the stage became a mission for Roy. He spent hours helping to measure, saw, and hammer the stage together after school with a small group of "carpenters" in Room 114. He found a niche into which he fit and quickly gained the respect of his heretofore reluctant classmates as they watched him help direct the construction of the stage. Roy didn't become a model student overnight but he certainly made strides toward becoming part of a learning community in which he had reason to be proud.

In the case of very reluctant students I've found that becoming a member of the community must occur before they can truly engage in literacy. Take, for example, a girl I'll call Sara. She was loud, pushy, and generally disliked by her peers. Even I had a difficult time warming up to her. When I asked her to take a part in a play Sara was hesitant, but she accepted the role. Once she got on stage, she became a different person; the kids saw the change immediately, and this "new" Sara eventually replaced the "old" in our classroom. On stage her loud voice became clear and well articulated, and she seemed to pour her pushy side into playing strong characters. The risks Sara took empowered her and brought out her positive traits. Two of these traits were her strong voice and good memory for lines. Thus, Sara joined our class as a reader and eventually as a contributing writer.

Conclusion

I am a much happier teacher than I was in my former classroom with its straight blinds and quiet, orderly students. Now when I hit a rough spot or simply get exhausted, I turn to reading good journals and talking with colleagues I respect. I find my teaching is evolving constantly. After decades of teaching I still search for my own strengths and those of the children. I am so much more child-centered, and this pleases me greatly. My own writing has also improved and grown along with the children's. In the past few years I've published poems, short stories, and teaching ideas in *Teaching K–8, Instructor,* and *Educational Leadership.*

Finally, I want to conclude with some advice. During my first week at C112 I had more anxiety than I ever experienced in the first year of my former teaching life. Fortunately, those of you educated today won't have to travel as far as I did. I took a long while to learn that one must define a philosophy and work to make it consistent with one's teaching. This is how to have a professional life. As a professional and more fulfilled person, I find I need all the more to reach out to professional organizations such as the National Council of Teachers of English. Various state and local conferences are also important. One needs to belong in these places as well as the classroom. Let professional books and journals become your mentors, too. You have everything to gain as you

> talk the talk
> and walk the walk
> sing more
> read more
> celebrate more
> share more
> care more about learning
> living a language-rich life
>
> J. George

For the Instructional Conversation

In-Class or In-Group Thinking, Writing, and Talking

1. Jack was unhappy in his early years of teaching. Skim the first few pages of his section and then write a short piece about the reasons he was not happy. Connect with one or two reasons by putting yourself in

his place. Talk with a peer and compare notes. Working together, do a written conversation (conduct in silence) and jot down some points on what you know about how school or district mandates operate now. Is what you know in conflict or agreement with Jack's experiences?

2. Brainstorm with others and develop a list of topics about which you might write a poem. Using poetic license, write a poem. (It doesn't have to rhyme!) Note how you felt before you began to write, what it felt like as you were writing, and how you felt when you were finished. Discuss with the class or group.

3. Write a one- or two-page letter to an administrator on the pros and cons of teachers having total control over what they teach. In groups of two to four people, switch papers, read, and then talk about the papers you've read and had read by another.

Reflective Thinking and Action

1. Using this section as a base and other resources, develop a miniportfolio on ways to teach poetry, a short list of poetry books for children, and at least one book for teachers. Describe a book you find particularly attractive, a poetry project you would like to try, and why you are attracted to the project.

   To extend: Swap your miniportfolio draft with a peer for feedback, and you provide feedback for your peer in like manner. Continue this swapping process until you think your portfolio is sufficiently developed for the final draft.

2. Write a paragraph to describe a person, situation, or event in your life. When the paragraph is complete, reread and begin to decide which words you can eliminate. Keep distilling the paragraph until you reach the essence of the idea. You will not have sentences, but you will have ideas. Share your work with someone as you work to discover if the nugget of your idea remains. Discuss the process of writing poetry in this way. Share with others.

Chapter Summary

Persistence is the word that most quickly comes to mind when thinking about the personal and professional journeys of Donna and Jack. Donna's experience in getting her degree and in finding the knowledge and context in which she could become her best teaching self has many challenges. In similar ways Jack experienced his own challenge in a deliberate move into constructivist learning theory. Both these teachers took significant risks in learning to teach and becoming part of the profession. Donna and Jack also resolved to develop their individual strengths for writing. Donna did and still does this with her journal writing, and her journals generate new ideas and endeavors. Jack is a member of a poetry group, which led him to become a poet as well as a better teacher of poetry. Donna and Jack's journeys are not highly unusual. Many teachers desire similar changes and personal growth. Other teachers also take significant risks to find the "growing room" they must have to hone their beliefs and develop better practice. Of the many characteristics of effective teachers, persistence and desire seem essential. Donna and Jack are good examples of effective teachers. They demonstrate that

- Resources and teacher learning coalesce; e.g., once they found the resource, in this case a supportive context, these two teachers' learning skyrocketed.

- Specific factors help teachers acquire and sustain positive and well-informed journeys toward learning to teach, e.g., their desire to teach in personally fulfilling ways.

- Finding a place of belonging in teaching is critical to feeling good about one's work; e.g., Donna and Jack found a place in which they belonged in a community of administrators and teachers.

References

Allen, J., and J. Mason. 1992. *Risk Makers; Risk Takers; Risk Breakers.* Portsmouth, N.H.: Heinemann.

Atwell, N. 1998. *In the Middle.* Portsmouth, N.H.: Heinemann.

Avery, C. 1985. *And With a Light Touch.* Portsmouth, N.H.: Heinemann.

Baylor, B. 1995. *I'm in Charge of Celebrations.* New York: Simon and Schuster.

Calkins, L. 1994. *The Art of Teaching Writing.* Portsmouth, N.H.: Heinemann.

Cowley, J. 1993. *The Screaming Mean Machine.* New York: Scholastic.

Gentry, J., and J. Gillet. 1993. *Teaching Kids to Spell.* Portsmouth, N.H.: Heinemann.

Goodman, Y., and S. Wilde, eds. 1992. *Literacy Events in a Community of Young Writers.* New York: Teachers College Press.

Graves, D. 1983. *Writing: Teachers and Children at Work.* Portsmouth, N.H.: Heinemann.

Hansen, J. 1992. "Anna Evaluates Herself." In *Risk Makers; Risk Takers; Risk Breakers,* eds. J. Allen & J. Mason. 19–29. Portsmouth, N.H.: Heinemann.

Holdway, D. 1979. *The Foundations of Literacy.* Gosford, N.S.W.: Ashton Scholastic.

McClung, R. 1990. *Hugh Glass Mountain Man.* New York: Morrow Junior.

Ministery of Education, N.Z. 1992. *Dancing With the Pen: The Learner as a Writer* Wellington, N.Z.: Learning Media, Ministry of Education.

Nash, O. 1997. *Under Water with Ogden Nash.* New York: Curtis Brown and London: Carlton Books.

Routman, R. 1991. *Invitations: Changing as Teachers and Learners, K–12.* Portsmouth, N.H.: Heinemann.

Ryland, C. 1985. *When I was Young in the Mountains.* New York: Dutton Child.

Silverstein, S. 1974. *Where the Sidewalk Ends.* New York: Harper & Row Junior Books.

Vygotsky, L. 1978. *Mind in Society: The Development of Higher Psychological Processes.* Cambridge, Mass.: Harvard University Press.

Wilde, S. 1992. *You Kan Red This.* Portsmouth, N.H.: Heinemann.

Jack George's Recommended Books

Brown, M. 1985. *Hand Rhymes.* New York: Dutton Children's Books.

Colgin, M. 1982. *One Potato, Two Potato, Three Potato, Four.* Mt. Ranier, Md.: Gryphon House.

Florian, D. 1999. *Laugh-eteria.* San Diego, Calif.: Harcourt Brace

Lansky, B. 1999. *Miles of Smiles.* Minnetonka, Minn.: Meadowbrook.

Prelutsky, J. 1991. *For Laughing Out Loud.* New York: Knopf.

Prelutsky. 1999. *A Pizza the Size of the Sun.* New York: Greenwillow.

Shields, C. 1995. *Lunch Money.* New York: Dutton Child.

4

Writing in Math and Science

WITH CONTRIBUTIONS BY
KRIS GREGORY AND PHYLLIS WHITIN

Effective instruction includes writing and reading in all subjects, not just language arts. Children learn a great deal when they write about science, mathematics, social studies, and other subjects. In this chapter, Kris Gregory and Phyllis Whitin share their expertise in showing how they teach math and science through writing. Their work also reveals the inner strength that drives good teaching. Kris' and Phyllis' caring and principled instruction, inner dialogue, and application of research also help to illustrate the ways in which a teacher and his or her teaching can change, grow, and become more theory-based.

These teachers' professional developments were influenced by learning from multiple sources; however, for both of them university courses made a significant difference. For example, Kris' graduate classes literally changed her teaching life. The events leading up to taking that graduate course and those that followed mapped the route for Kris' learning. Having traveled the path of enjoying math and gaining true understanding, she is forever changed through deeper understanding. In Phyllis' case, her discussion in Chapter 1 explains a course experience that introduced her to a playfulness toward math and inspiration for math that she had not known. In addition, that course and its all-important instructor helped Phyllis gain true understanding of mathematical concepts and what it takes to teach them.

Kris Gregory

Kris Gregory: *Writing Mathematics and Science in a Multiage Classroom*

Kris Gregory teaches in a rural/suburban school in the same state as John Green-well and JoAnn Archie. Kris' school serves a large population of white Appalachian, low-income children.

My journey toward learning to teach through problem solving began when I was very young. I grew up surrounded by strong, visionary teachers. My grandmother, grandfather, mother, aunt, and many close family friends all helped shape my life and my views of education and learning. My grandmother was a child-centered teacher. Grandmother told stories; one of her favorite topics was the adventures she had while mentoring families through Head Start. She brought meaningful print to families' homes, including newspapers and community information, and she was their guide to literacy through local theater and the library. She made literacy authentic and personal.

Both my parents were outstanding teachers (no bias on my part!). Mom taught school and Dad introduced us to literature and other cultures. Dad liked to involve my brothers and me in his electronic restoration projects. From this I learned the fundamental value of problem solving through hands-on projects. At home my learning was real, active, and meaningful.

At school, my learning was exactly the opposite. For the first six years of school, math made no sense to me at all. I was the child I discussed in Chapter 1—the one who held the damp and smelly work sheet with trembling hands. To me math was a foreign language. Fortunately, my father was there to translate and help me make sense of the meaningless numbers and symbols. After supper we would sit at the kitchen table under the warm light of the tulip lamp and make our way. My father helped me understand math problems and how they could be solved in different ways.

I remember the first time I had a flash of understanding and finally "got" long division. I solved every homework problem correctly and verified each answer. At school the next day I proudly turned in my paper. At the end of the day my teacher returned it to me. The whole paper was a sea of angry red slashes and words! I couldn't believe it. Because I hadn't solved the problem the way we did them in class, she had marked every one wrong.

Facing the Realities of Teaching and Finding Another Way

In my own first-grade classroom many years later, I ended up doing what teachers do when they have not yet gained sufficient knowledge and confidence—I followed what the other teachers did. Slowly, without realizing it, I was teaching as I'd been taught. This in spite of my vow! I used workbooks and even some dreaded work sheets.

My students groaned when I announced it was math time. I knew I *had* to change. I worked at it and became more confident in the act of trying out new ideas. My first break with tradition was telling my students to get out their crayons and draw pictures to represent objects being added in addition problems. This was a very small step but a meaningful one. Then we used the crayons themselves and other physical objects to help solve problems. About this time I attended a math workshop and took a graduate course that greatly changed my thinking about math. In the workshop the professor demonstrated how to use real objects to make math more meaningful, and he emphasized how important it is for children to talk about math and how they figure out problems. In the graduate course we read *Innumeracy: Mathematical Illiteracy and its Consequences* (Paulos 2000).

Paulos' point is that because school mathematics instruction is often focused on skills and drills, people don't learn to analyze or solve problems involving numbers. I also read *Making Sense: Teaching and learning mathematics with understanding* (1997, 1), which influenced me greatly.

> In order to take advantage of new opportunities and to meet the challenges of tomorrow, today's students need flexible approaches for defining and solving problems. They need problem-solving methods that can be adapted to new situations, and they need the know-how to develop new methods for new kinds of problems.

Another event in graduate school added length to my stride toward learning to teach. I read a book called *Other People's Words* by Victoria Purcell-Gates (1996). I was fascinated to read about the themes of child-centered, authentic teaching and the importance of literacy in a family's life. This book focused on literacy much as my grandmother had many years before. I felt empowered.

To prepare for a statewide reform and for multiage teaching, my fellow teachers and I studied, attended workshops, and took classes. We collaborated and visited effective teachers in their classrooms. I went to see a teacher named Marianne Davis, and her teaching made a profound impression on me. I promised myself I was going to create a classroom as warm, inviting, stimulating, and literacy-rich as hers. Shortly after visiting Marianne Davis I made a move to a multiage classroom, grades three and four.

During this period my classroom changed rapidly, and it continues to change to this day. I worked to empower children by being more open. I provided for ownership through classroom discussion and student self-selection. Such changes required new management thinking and strategies for the children and me. As these changes unfolded, I began to focus on mathematical problem solving and the language of mathematics.

Mathematics in Our Classroom

In my multiage classroom one of my goals is to have children help each other construct understandings of complex mathematical concepts and use writing to reflect on their learning. The following example of Hanna's math journal shows that the children benefited from working together.

> Today I was doing math with my best friend Abigail. We were doing regrouping. It was hard. She looked at me and said, "Do you need help?" I said "Yes, Please!" So she helped me understand. I felt good about it. In fact I only missed one or two. I was glad she helped me. (Journal entry, Hanna, eight years old)

Every day Abigail, Hanna, and the other children in our classroom are busy reading, writing, listening, sharing, presenting, and using what they've learned to solve problems, ask new questions, and make sense of the world around them. Believe me, my teaching wasn't always this way. My journey toward problem solving and a language arts focus in mathematics took some "scary" steps.

From the beginning of the school year, I explain to my students why I teach problem solving and divergent thinking. I tell them that we are going to learn to use metacognition. This is the ability to think about and verbalize thinking processes so someone else can see what you are thinking. I deliberately and consistently think out loud as I model mathematical thinking and solve math problems on an overhead projector. Some of my students are naturally good at thinking out loud from the very start. Taking their lead and mine, others soon engage in thinking out loud as they work on math.

Children often learn more quickly from each other than they do from me. I put them in small groups so they can discuss the different strategies and processes they use to solve problems. I find that multiability groups work well (as long as the range is not too wide). Other teaching steps go something like this:

- I teach students to write down their thoughts and processes using numbers, symbols, and words in math language.
- I set aside a time every day for children to explore and discuss numbers, concepts, strategies, manipulatives, and processes.
- We brainstorm and post reflective questions on large chart paper to keep focused. Some examples we generate are:

What is my answer?	How did I solve the problem?
What was my plan?	Is my answer reasonable?
What strategy did I use?	Why did I choose this strategy?

As the children work and talk, I see how important it is to help them make their learning concrete and visible through talk and writing together. My math program is anchored in problem solving and children's use of math language to justify and explain their work. Students create posters to illustrate the steps to problem solving, the ways of organizing information, and kinds of useful reflective questions. These posters serve as a good reminder for at least the first half of the school year.

Writing Math on a Daily Basis

To learn the problem-solving process, we need easy access to problematic situations. Here is an example.

We posed the following question: How many noses are in our room? As we worked, we quickly discovered a problem: the children couldn't determine how many people were in the room! We ran out of time trying. At first I felt this lesson had bombed and didn't know what to do about it. I talked with my team teacher and, most importantly, with my students about it. Then I realized that I had to leave the problem up to the students. Rather than showing children how to solve the problem, I suggested that *they* brainstorm to find out how to solve this problem. Jenny suggested using their names on their mailboxes, other children suggested names on the lunch board, and various other ways to count the number of people. They even came up with a system to show whom we had counted and whom we had not—e.g., with tally marks, colored dots, and post-it notes with names of students. One child actually got some clay, made noses, and handed them out. This event was critical for me because I had trusted the children *and* my beliefs. The students' ability to talk through this problem and build on each other's ideas was exciting. They could hardly wait for math the next day so they could tackle this problem! This kind of response builds courage and takes the anxiety out of doing math. Here is another example of a problem we had fun with.

At our Valentine's Day party, fifteen students in our class brought Valentine cards and exchanged cards with every person in our class. How many Valentine cards did we have in our classroom? How many exchanges would that be? After we read the problem and made sure we understood it, we wrote down the important information we needed to know to solve the problem:

- There were fifteen children.
- Every child exchanged Valentine's cards with every other child.
- We had to figure out how many Valentine's cards each child brought.
- We had to know what an exchange meant for this problem.

Finally, we thought about other problems we'd done that were like this and how we solved them. We decided it seemed a lot like the handshake problem we had solved the week before: if there are five people, how many times will each person shake hands with a different person? One of the third-graders, Simon, remembered that we solved that problem by acting it out and by drawing a picture. The class voted to act out the Valentine problem, using five people instead of fifteen. We found leftover Valentine's cards and physically enacted the problem. Fred stood at the marker board and recorded the number of Valentine cards and the number of exchanges that took place. Penny Jo attempted to draw a diagram on the board of the five exchanges. It got complicated, so several children, with my guidance, got up and acted it out again with only two people. Then everyone drew a picture representing that part of the problem. Some students noticed that for every two Valentine cards, there was one exchange. Once Fischer verbalized this to the class, the children began solving the problem. After some guidance and discussion about problem-solving procedures and guidelines, the class got to work in the following ways:

- Children worked individually and in pairs.
- Everyone was engaged in active problem solving.

- Children shared the materials, processes, procedures, organizational strategies, and operations they used.
- Later in the day I recorded several children's responses, and the next day during shared reading time we read and discussed them.
- I focused my teaching on showing children what they knew.

Class sharing helps students understand their own thinking and explain their thinking more clearly. The results are powerful. This interaction comes after weeks of solving problems and engaging in instructional conversations about the language, strategies, and processes we use. I provide a great deal of whole-class and small-group support before I ask children to be independent in their work. This is the right thing to do for their sake and mine—it helps prevent behavior problems. Children usually don't act out if they feel safe in what teachers ask them to do. So it is up to teachers to provide enough support and structure for children to feel safe. Good behavior nearly always results. Here's an example of a more advanced problem.

> In a recent survey at our school, twenty people out of fifty people had blond hair. If there are six hundred people in our school, how many of them probably have blond hair? Be sure to explain how you solved the problem, why you chose your plan, and what you learned.

I chose this problem because it could be solved using many of the same strategies the children used with the Valentine's card problem. For example, they could use multiplication, drawing objects to make the abstract concrete, repeated addition, and ratios. At this point, instead of demonstrating the problem-solving steps comprehensively, I review only briefly and then send the children off to solve the problem. I observe them and determine how well they can use problem-solving strategies on their own. I intervene and teach as needed for every child's success.

As you can see from the sample of children's responses in Figure 4–1, they were able to solve the problem successfully, and explain their strategies. I am always amazed at what eight- to ten-year-old children can do when they receive the support they need. When I compare it with my own math instruction at the same age, I'm ever grateful that I no longer teach the way I was taught.

Writing in Science

I know my children can write, study, and learn from their responses to literature and to math in other subjects. Thus, I teach and assess by integrating language arts and problem solving in science. Here is an example of how one of our science projects went.

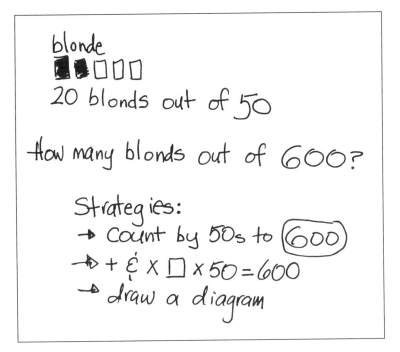

blonde

20 blonds out of 50

How many blonds out of 600?

Strategies:
→ Count by 50s to (600)
→ + $\acute{e}$ X ☐ x 50 = 600
→ draw a diagram

Figure 4–1.

We studied the rain forest, and the children became fascinated with the many and varied adaptations animals have made to survive. To build on their interests and give them a framework and focus for writing, I developed the following task:

Situation: Discuss the following. There are four layers of rain forest. Different animals live in each layer. To survive they have developed special features and adaptations.
Writing Task: In your letter to a friend, choose a layer of the rain forest and an animal that lives there. Explain to your friend how the animal has adapted its body and its habits to survive in that layer. Give specific details to support your explanation.

I am as concerned about state and district standards as any teacher. So, using our state format, I have a scoring rubric for the assigned task. I share it with my class before they begin writing. I develop assessments that fit with almost any school standards. I recommend that teachers do this as they plan and implement instruction. It saves headaches and work, and you'll never have to worry about defending your practice once you get in the habit.

Rubric for Rain Forest Letters

Distinguished

Establishes purpose in elaborate or creative way. Uses sophisticated language to communicate with audience. Facts included are written in engaging ways, with elaborate, important details. The piece is highly organized and skills are used effectively.

Proficient

Establishes purpose of introducing a rain forest animal to a friend. Communicates with audience. Facts are supported with elaborate, important details. Piece shows some organization. A few surface errors are evident.

Apprentice

Establishes purposes in simplistic way (may be unclear). Some attempt to communicate with audience. Facts are given in list form with simple repetitious or unrelated details. May lapse in focus or organization. May have several surface errors.

Novice

May not establish purpose. Little awareness of audience. Facts in list form with few or no details. Piece is unorganized and unfocused. Errors may get in the way of meaning.

After students received the rain forest problem, they read reference books, magazines, and encyclopedias and visited related websites and media encyclopedias. Their work was much like the theme-cycling and inquiry instruction described by Ruth and John in Chapter 2. As they gathered information, the students began prewriting and organizing their ideas. Students engaged in the following:

- wrote a rough draft and conferred with a classmate
- confirmed that their writing was clear and focused
- checked with others and me on the following criteria: writing included adaptations of their animal, e.g., how the animal survived, and gave details to interest the (peer) reader

After revisions and editing, children used the rubric to self-assess, gave themselves a score, and justified their decision. I also score their pieces and write notes to explain my score. I copied students' pieces, and during the rest of the week we read and studied them. Then they had the opportunity to draft a final copy.

Because the rain forest and its living organisms become real for these children, most are impassioned. Their literacy and learning is genuine and meaningful. Our culminating activity is a trip to a miniature rain forest at the local zoo. This trip sparks further interest and opportunities for learning. Once children become comfortable with a curriculum cycle of reading, writing, and problem solving, their learning becomes self-sustaining. This most happy situation takes a great burden off the teacher because one learning event leads naturally to the next. Teaching this way is much less stressful. In fact, it becomes the creative, satisfying, and intellectual experience it should be!

Conclusion

One of the most important things I continue to learn in my work is how to establish and maintain good relationships with children. I know that if I don't build a climate of trust and mutual respect, my teaching will not be nearly as effective as it is. It's also vital for me to keep up with thought-provoking books and articles. Discussing my readings with friends is as important as the reading. My professional friends and I always end up talking about teaching and learning even when we go out to dinner. It's stimulating and empowering to have these relationships.

Bill Ayers (1993, 127) helps me sum up how I feel about my work.

> The work of a teacher—exhausting, complex, idiosyncratic, never twice the same—is, at its heart, an intellectual and ethical enterprise. Teaching is the vocation of vocations, a calling that shepherds a multitude of other callings. It is an activity that is intensely practical and yet transcendental, brutally matter of fact, and yet fundamentally a creative act. Teaching begins as a challenge and is never far from mystery. Teaching is a fascinating, lifelong journey; one that will continue in the hearts and minds of those you touch. Tread lightly.

For the Instructional Conversation

In-Class or In-Group Thinking, Writing, and Talking

1. On your own look through Kris' section and identify instances of math language use. Make a dual-entry journal by drawing a vertical line down the middle of a piece of paper. Write the math language

phrase on the left and jot down a question or comment on the right side. The dual-entry journal is meant to be quick. Turn to a peer and compare and contrast your entries. Note why the use of math language may be good for learning. Discuss your views with others.

2. Have you had a classroom experience in which you felt as Kris did when the teacher marked her paper with a sea of angry red slashes? Consider the circumstances of this event (any school incident that caused you hurt or embarrassment) and write a short piece listing your age, the subject matter, and any details you can recall, such as visual images, smells, colors, or look of the classroom. Then quickly write a list of words that help capture how you felt. Your responses might become a poem or remain in this form. Share with others.

3. Review the physical artifacts and the collaborative interactions Kris uses to provide scaffolding. Using the dual-entry journal technique again, write down the artifact or event on the left side of the vertical line on your paper and your "unpacking," or analysis of the artifact or event on the right side. On the right side, show what makes it a scaffold. If you wish, use the following categories from Tharp and Gallimore to describe the scaffolding properties. When you are finished, share your findings with another person or with the whole group. Scaffolding categories are joint problem solving, intersubjectivity (come to shared understandings), warmth and responsiveness (creating a positive tone, providing verbal praise, attributing competence to the child), and promoting self-regulation (stepping back to let children take control of their own activity, providing assistance as needed).

Reflective Thinking and Action

1. Kris mentions several books in her section. As you wish, read any of these books and set up a What do you know about this topic? What do you want to learn? and What have you learned? (KWL). Write down what you think you *know* about the book's content before you read it, write what you *want* to learn as you read the book, and finally write up what you have *learned* after you have finished reading. Try putting these three categories on separate pieces of paper. As you read, you might list new information or changes in the questions with which you began. Prepare a short presentation of the KWL on paper or overheads, or prepare a brief power point.

2. Kris assigned a writing topic in her rain forest science unit. This assignment seemed to work well for her and her students. Donna Ware's assigned writing topic (see p. 157) on friendship did not meet with student or teacher success. Reread Donna's and Kris' sections. Then prepare a short paper on the context and content of the assignments and why you think one worked and the other did not.

3. Kris had a teacher who either thought that emphasizing one way to solve a problem was good for children's learning *or* didn't understand that there were multiple ways of solving math problems. Consider this idea as you investigate the difficulties that some teachers have in teaching math. Your search can include any resources you wish. Journal articles, books, and interviews with other teachers work well. Develop an oral or written persuasion piece that takes a stand on why math has been and is still taught with a "one-way-to-solve-a-problem" approach.

Phyllis Whitin: *Reading, Writing, and Discovering in Math and Science*

Phyllis Whitin's teaching is set in South Carolina. Her students are heterogeneous, with a wide range of abilities. Phyllis' area of South Carolina is fairly flat, heat is plentiful, and schools are air-conditioned by necessity. Even in midwinter, days of forty degrees are interspersed with fairly balmy weather.

Phyllis Whitin

I'm grateful for the early influences in my learning. I remember the huge model grocery store my second-grade teacher helped the class to construct. We stocked the shelves with empty cans and boxes, priced items, and took turns buying groceries and tallying receipts at the toy cash registers. That experience was probably one of my earliest (and rarest) opportunities to connect mathematical learning to a meaningful context. My third-grade teacher provided time in our weekly schedule for groups of children to meet in clubs centered on an interest. I was part of a science club, and I still remember researching turtles. This teacher also sparked an interest in astronomy, and one of my first treasured read-for-pleasure books was *The Golden Book of Stars*, which I still own! As I reflect on these early experiences, I realize the joy in my learning came from my experiences in connecting my schoolwork to a functional context in my own life. Perhaps the roots of my current interest in interdisciplinary teaching lie firmly embedded in my own childhood.

Embarking on My Career

Carolyn Burke refers to educators as professional learners rather than teachers. I agree. With the help of professional colleagues (through reading, conferences, workshops, etc.) and the children themselves, I've become more and more excited about finding ways to integrate math, science, reading, and writing.

During my teacher training experiences in the 1970s, the British Primary Schools, with their child-centered and progressive philosophy, influenced American education. I incorporated some of their ideas in my initial elementary teaching: using math manipulatives and math in real contexts and writing descriptive commentaries about work produced in various subject areas (art, math, science, etc.). This early practice grounded my appreciation for writing across the curriculum. However, I can see missed potential:

- The focus of the writing was a description of the product; it was not about the process of thinking.
- Although I posted the children's work on the bulletin board, the audience for their writing was quite limited.
- I didn't provide time for children to talk in an exploratory way. Neither talking nor writing was a tool for discovery. Immersion in the writing process opened new doors for me (Graves 1983).

Writing Process Lessons from Middle School

After teaching third grade and preschool, I relocated to another state. The only teaching job I could find was a language arts position at the middle-school level. I was disappointed (and nervous), but, in a serendipitous set of circumstances that teaching often holds, I found that this context of teaching afforded me some wonderful opportunities to learn about learning—and to learn about writing in math and science.

I devoted a great deal of time reading about the writing process and attending workshops. At one writing conference, Donald Murray taught me one of my most significant lessons about teaching and learning. He asked the participants to free-write, stop, reread our work, and raise our hands if we had written something that we had not originally intended to write. As hands filled the air, he explained that writers "write to discover what they have to say" (Murray 1967, 9). I was excited about this notion of writing as a tool for discovery, and it has influenced my teaching ever since. Taking his lead, I began to ask my students to reread their work and note places of discovery. I didn't know it at the time, but I would later learn to apply this idea to writing about math and science as well.

Another key idea of a writers' workshop is the importance of publishing for a wide range of purposes. That idea, too, had been missing in my early years of teaching. As I read more and listened to the children's interests more closely, I realized that I needed to broaden the range of writing topics that I offered. I was concentrating too heavily on narratives. In looking for new writing topics and audiences, I discovered ways to integrate math, science, and writing. Two of the most successful projects were math-science stories for young children and consumer issues studies.

Writing Math-Science Stories for Young Children

While filling in student record forms, I noticed that one student's mother taught at a nearby nursery school. I asked if the seventh-graders could write simple, predictable books for her class. She agreed, and my pen-pal project was born. The "big kids" studied picture books with predictable formats, such as counting books and books that followed familiar sequences such as the days of the week. They wrote, conferred with their classmates and me, revised, created dummy layouts, edited, illustrated, and bound their books. We set a date for our visit, practiced reading the books aloud, and finally met the preschoolers. What a joyous day! I also saw a new side of some of my most challenging students. Their enthusiasm (and their honest comments) inspired me to expand the program to a full-year pen-pal project with primary children, in which the students corresponded, read, and wrote together.

When we worked with this older audience, I began to use a wider range of children's literature with a mathematical focus as inspirations for the student-made books. One important reference for these books was *Read Any Good Math Lately?* (Whitin 1992). Many of the books that we used integrated mathematics and science topics. Some of my favorites are:

How Much is A Million? (Schwartz 1985)

Counting on Frank (Clement 1991)

Large as Life Animals (Cole 1985)

If You Hopped Like a Frog (Schwartz 1999)

One Grain of Rice (Demi 1997)

A Remainder of One (Pinczes 1995)

Sea Square (Hulme 1993)

Bat Jamboree (Appelt 1996)

So Many Circles, So Many Squares (Hoban 1998)

The Big Bug Book (Facklan 1994)

The project had the following format:

- Work with primary teachers to match up pen pals.
- Write letters to younger children about school, personal interests, etc. (about once a month).
- Set a date for a reading celebration.
- Read and study published picture books for style and format.
- Write, share, and revise stories.
- Visit the primary classrooms for paired reading.

One of our pen-pal projects followed the pattern of Cole's *Large as Life Animals.* The author describes interesting animals by comparing their size and shape to more familiar objects. The royal antelope, for example, is so tiny that all four of its hooves could fit on a half-dollar. The students discussed how Cole's use of benchmarks enabled the reader to picture the different animals. I invited the class to write a story about an animal for their pen pals and to include statistical information. It was challenging for them to find mathematical comparisons that a six-year-old could understand. We generated a list as a group. Some common items used as comparisons included toothpaste cap, a basketball, a chalkboard eraser, a sticker, and a lunchbox. While talking and writing, the students discovered other ideas (just as Don Murray had showed me). Here is Kenneth's final story:

> Some large dolphins can reach up to 15 feet long. That's as long as a station wagon. Dolphins can swim up to 25 miles an hour. That's how fast you drive in a neighborhood. Dolphins get up to 400 pounds. Dolphins are mammals. They have a hole in the top of their heads to breathe with.
>
> A dolphin sends messages under water with high pitch noises. That's like us on the telephone. Dolphins eat mainly squid and marine life. Dolphins are neat-o.

When I asked Kenneth how he thought of these comparisons, he explained that he had talked to his classmate and close friend, Ryan. The two boys lived in the same neighborhood, and Ryan's family had a station wagon. Once they thought of the station wagon for length, they built on that idea and they used it again for a benchmark for speed. Collaborating with his friend had encouraged Kenneth to generate new ideas. Notice that Kenneth wrote about dolphins' form of communication. When I asked him about that idea, he explained that he had been thinking about his older sister and how much time she spent talking on the telephone. I think this comparison shows that writers do draw on personal experiences!

The pen-pal projects helped me and my students enlarge our view of descriptive writing. Nonfiction writing shares the same key elements as fiction: clarity, attention to detail, and careful word choice. Publishing is key, too: students invested a great deal of thought and energy into their stories because they wrote for a specific audience.

Consumer Issues Projects

Authors write best about topics that are important to them. Short and Harste (1996, 51) state, "[An] alternative way to organize curriculum is around inquiry questions of personal and social interest." Exploring consumer issues allows the students to connect their real-life experiences of shopping with their characteristic sense of fairness. This project uses mathematics in a real context (Whitin 1992) and helps develop a healthy skepticism toward the kinds of numerical data used in advertising. The project followed this general outline:

- Invite students to tell stories about incidents when they felt cheated by stores.
- Cluster the stories by topic.

- Engage in further discussions about product guarantees, telephone shopping, advertising gimmicks, and consumer rights. *Smart Spending: A Young Consumer's Guide* (Schmitt 1989) is a good resource.
- Study magazine and newspaper advertisements for techniques such as word choice, strategic use of fine print, and numerical data (such as showing the cost per payment rather than the total cost of a car).
- Brainstorm topics for further investigation.
- Choose topics for research (individual or small-group).
- Submit a project proposal (see the Appendix) that details methods for gathering data, print and nonprint resources, and a final project design (charts, pictures, written texts, letters of complaint, etc.).
- Implement the research, using class time for the sharing of drafts.
- Present findings to the class.

Research projects such as this one can connect home and school nicely, as in the case of Brent, who was a hesitant writer. Brent worked with his dad, who had been in retail sales for twenty years. The two visited several stores together, comparing prices of products. They found the price of a particular brand of aspirin at a local hotel guest shop, a discount store, a grocery store, and a convenience store. During his investigation, Brent raised ethical questions. When he found the hotel price to be much higher, he asked the hotel personnel where they purchased their goods. They named a discount store. Brent worried, "I wondered why it's not a crime to be able to charge all that? How can they go out and buy, and then resell it for that price?"

Brent's father also taught him gimmicks such as *leaders* (using a low price on one item to lure customers to a store for general purchases) and terminology such as *bulk sales* and *captive market*. Through his project, Brent learned that both math and language are value-laden. He was becoming a concerned citizen as well as a more informed shopper.

Michael and Jeff picked a seemingly bland topic: which restaurants in our area had the most business on Sunday noon. The lesson they taught me (as well as each other), however, was that real inquiry involves defining a problem, examining data from multiple perspectives, and drawing conclusions. After telephoning several restaurants (followed by on-site visits if they weren't taken seriously), they decided to plot the restaurants on a map, using colors to indicate the popularity of different restaurants. Showing their data in this way enabled them to discover a relationship between the location of popular restaurants and churches. They concluded that sit-down restaurants located conveniently near churches did the most business on Sundays. Take-out restaurants, even those close to churches, did not show any advantage over restaurants further away. Like Brent, these boys raised new questions to consider even as they concluded their project: How would our results change if we gathered data on Fridays? Mondays?

I asked Michael to contrast the role of mathematics in this project with regular math class. He explained:

> [In math class] you've got the problems right there. When you've got tests and worksheets like that, you've got your own problems already there, and you have to figure out the answer. But when you do this kind of project you get information and make your own problem up. You're making up your own problem, and you're learning how to do it . . . you're solving it.

It was important to Michael that he made up his own problem. Not only did the boys choose their topic, they had to create ways to gather, tabulate, and interpret their data. Michael and his partner connected mathematical tools with map-making from social studies and with interviewing, reading, and writing in language arts. By creating their own problem and inventing ways to solve it, the boys were empowered.

My teaching in middle school (a job that at first disappointed me) was rewarding and purposeful. Though I did not stay in middle school, I learned a lot from students such as Michael. I was beginning to understand the connection between thinking like a writer and thinking like a mathematician or scientist. Personal voice, choice of topics, real purposes, and creation of shape and form are common elements in all acts of authoring.

Research, Writing, and Scientific Learning with Fourth-graders

Broad themes such as consumerism and genre studies such as picture books have great potential for writers' workshop projects. Sometimes themes emerge almost unintentionally, which is what happened in my new fourth-grade classroom. Here is how it happened.

When I transferred to an elementary school in my district, I was assigned to a portable classroom. Portables, with their noisy heaters and cramped quarters, make classroom conversation problematic. They are often leaky in rainy weather. But, the best thing about my portable was the setting—it was located in a grassy courtyard with small ornamental trees. I hung a bird feeder full of seed and a hummingbird feeder in a crabapple tree just outside the window. The bird feeders led the children and me into a powerful long-term project that incorporated scientific writing into our writers' workshop (and across all subjects in the curriculum). Here are the steps I took at the beginning of the project:

- Invite one child at a time to observe at the window for a brief period each day. Have the child write and draw in a class community journal. (Draw a name at random. Children may decline the invitation. I also have learned that with any new project, starting slowly keeps me from feeling overwhelmed with the unknown.)

- Provide time for the observer of the day to report his or her findings to the class during a designated sharing time.

- Conduct brief classroom discussions about the child's findings, using a format similar to authors' circles. (What do you find interesting about the child's observation? What do you want to know more about?) Take notes while the children talk.

- Record key observations and questions on chart paper. Post the paper near the window for ongoing comments and additions. *Doing What Scientists Do* (Doris 1991) was very helpful in guiding my role as teacher. I starred and reread several quotes in her book:

> Extending the initial observations children make at the science table is important—pointing out a puzzle or helping children frame a question is the first step in extending work. Then we need to help children figure out how to work on the question. Where can you find information? What kind of people can help? What kinds of books? How do you take a closer look? (Doris 1991, 93–94). When we hand children's questions back to them to answer, and they intently go off to "have another look," or breathlessly return to share their latest findings, then we have been helpful. If they seem confused, frustrated, or impatient with us, then perhaps the situation calls for another response (Doris 1991, 87).

Doris also discusses the importance of building a respectful classroom community.

Children need to feel safe to take risks in sharing their drawings and writing in science, just as they do in writers' workshop.

On the very first day of school the children and I read *Crow Boy* (Yashima 1955) to help set a "no-put-down" rule. It was important to establish this ground rule before any child brought an observation to the class for discussion.

The children noticed the bird feeders on the first day of school, and by the third day their interest was high. Bobby was the first child chosen to observe. He sat by the window and wrote a simple observation: "I saw a hummingbird eat some food." When he shared his writing with the class, no one criticized him for the brevity of his piece. I asked the class to tell Bobby what they liked about his observation ("I'm glad that you told that the humming-bird was eating."). Next they asked him questions (such as "How long did it eat?"). This pattern of first telling the observer what they appreciated and then continuing with questions such as, "I was interested in. . . . Could you say some more about that part?" worked well. The questions that children asked Bobby influenced the later bird reporters' entries. This was the same tech-nique I used in writers' workshop in middle school. Starting with a positive comment encourages writers of any age to take more risks in writing. It's im-portant to establish this routine early in the year with all writing—scientific or mathematical—with interviews, response to literature, and so on.

Rebecca was the next person to observe. She wrote:

> I saw two hummingbirds fighting over the hummingbird feeder. And they came back. I saw a bird nest in the tree. One came back and drank up and down seventeen times. They came back. The same two.

When Rebecca read her observation during our class sharing time, I took notes so I could learn from our experiences. I wondered if she added more details about eating based on the questions that were raised during Bobby's report. Rebecca's classmates complimented her on her careful obser-vation of the surrounding area (the nest) and her precision in counting the number of sips the hummingbird took. The children also had questions for Rebecca. Sam asked about the color of the birds. Rebecca had noticed their "reddish and blackish" color, but she had not included this information in her description. Sam's query demonstrated that in order to write more clearly for this audience, it was important to include information about color. Already the children were becoming more careful scientific writers. Raising the issue influenced the next journal observers.

Class discussions over the next several days raised many potential ques-tions to pursue. Initially, the questions focused on hummingbirds:

- Do hummingbirds really fight?
- Is it possible to distinguish individual characteristics within the same species, so that the same two birds can be identified?
- Will we see hummingbirds in the winter? Don't they leave? Where do they go?
- Why do they eat sugar water and other birds eat seeds?

Another job for the teacher (although the children joined in) is to pro-vide materials to support their inquiry, for instance, by checking out a collec-tion of books from the local library and providing time to read them (silent reading time works well). One outstanding book I found was a child's picture book: *Hummingbirds: Jewels of the Sky* (Tyrell 1986). One of the students brought in Tyrell's adult text, *Hummingbirds: Their Life and Behavior A Photographic Study of the North American Species* (1985). When children are interested, books have no level. We collected facts gleaned from reading and posted a list, Interesting Hummingbird Facts, by the window. Making each child's knowledge accessible for everyone in the class was key to the momentum of the project. Interestingly, many of the facts were mathematical in nature.

- Hummingbirds can flap their wings seventy eight times a second.
- The hummingbird's nest is the size of a dollhouse teacup.
- Hummingbirds don't sip to drink. They lap like a kitten. They lap thirteen times a second.

Instead of math needing to be fit into our writing, it arose quite naturally. By now several of the children begged for more time to pursue their research. Following their lead, I added bird observations as a choice during writers' workshop. Not all children wrote about birds. I feel that keeping the element of choice in the project was a key to its success. I learned about other aspects of choice, too. Sometimes I tried to nudge the children to follow a question for further research, and they showed no interest. Other times their questions totally surprised me, and off they went to find out more. I again thought about Doris' advice: "If a question is important to a child, then it is a good question to pursue. As teachers, we have to keep this in mind, for the questions children raise are not always the ones we would raise for them" (Doris 1991, 89).

To broaden the project, I followed these steps:

- Expand observation time during writers' workshop.
- Create a chart that organizes these observations (five or six children each day for five days a week; children are not required to observe).
- Develop a collection of rough drafts and drawings, and use these in discussions (just as adult scientists use their notes).
- Conduct minilessons that guide the children's use of their own voices in nonfiction texts (Harvey 1998).

I used two main sources to demonstrate the idea of voice in students' nonfiction writing: a piece of student writing that sounded natural and conversational and children's literature. For example, I read *The Trumpet of the Swan* (White 1970) aloud. Reading this book opened a door for writing fiction, something I had not anticipated when I began the bird project. As we read, the children became aware of the amount of research White had to do in order to write fiction. They were impressed with the inclusion of such facts as the swan's eight-foot wing span or, for some, their migration to the Red Rocks Lakes in Montana. The children wondered how much of the book was true. They spontaneously checked parts of the story with information in the field guides and nonfiction books that we had in class.

Soon several children began to write their own fictitious stories that incorporated scientific facts. Rick and Alex, who loved to entertain their classmates, collaborated on a story they entitled "Last Action Swan." At the conclusion of their story, they included facts about swans and their nesting habits. Again, writing in this alternative genre helped the children transform their factual knowledge in their own voices. Their story (and other stories and poems that followed) reminded me of the middle-school pen pal projects, when the children incorporated facts into writing for entertainment. Although other children wrote pieces that were clearly nonfiction, I learned to think more broadly about writing in mathematics and science.

Journals for Mathematical Thinking

In their scientific writing, different children noticed different things, and many of their observations were related to math. There was diversity in student thinking and writing. Writing about math computation, however, might seem more restrictive. How could I encourage children to write for their own understanding in math, especially in the traditionally narrow realm of computation? Recounting steps, such as "I put down the three and carried the one," does not help children reflect on their work and learn to think deeply about it. In thinking about this problem, I was facing an issue I had wondered about for some time. After some experimentation, I began to use math journals in order to foster a sense of ownership, individuality, and reflective thinking (Whitin and Whitin 2000). I started the year with noncomputational activities in math, such as geometric puzzles and classification games. Following a class discussion (talking as rehearsal is just as important in math as it is in any other writing), I asked the children to follow one or more of the following prompts in their journals, using writing and drawing:

- What do you notice?
- What was going through your head as you worked?
- What strategies did you invent to help you?
- What did you predict?
- What do you wonder about your discoveries now?

These open-ended prompts help the children show their thinking and support their personal voice or style of expression. The children shared their writing with each other, and I occasionally made an overhead transparency of some of their journals to highlight entries that showed thinking processes particularly well. I added additional prompts based upon the children's ways of expressing themselves (e.g., what surprised you about your discoveries?), and glued the list inside the front cover of their journals. This list became quite handy. When children became stuck, I often referred them to the list: "Look back at your journal questions and see which one is most helpful now."

Once I had established procedures for writing math journals, I thought it was time to turn to the more difficult issue of writing about computation. Here are some examples of how children used the prompts when solving subtraction problems using base blocks (math manipulatives consisting of *units,* or ones, *longs,* or tens, and *flats,* or 100s).

Using the prompt, "What was going through your head before you solved the problem?" Lisa explained how she estimated ahead of time in order to set a general idea for a reasonable answer. She also demonstrated a clear understanding of regrouping in the problem.

$$
\begin{array}{r}
500 \\
368 \\
\hline
132
\end{array}
\qquad
\begin{array}{r}
490 \\
500 \\
- \ 368 \\
\hline
132
\end{array}
$$

What I right off know is that there are two zeros on the top number and we will immediately go to the 5, and our answer will be less than 200 and greater than 100. After solving: I was right! The answer is lower than 200 and greater than 100. This subtraction problem is sort of like helping each number out so that it can subtract a number and get the answer.

Lisa's writing shows her personal style of explaining a problem. Lisa often described regrouping as a number "helping each number out." She also made her use of estimation clear. ("The answer will be less than 200 and greater than 100.") When she arrived at the final solution, she checked back to her original estimate. I found I could assess her understanding much better through her writing than by reading a sheet of computation practice.

Other children, such as Cody, showed their humor in their writing.

$$
\begin{array}{r}
174 \\
- \ 82 \\
\hline
92
\end{array}
$$

I took 4 units and took away two units, so I have two units. And I knew $7 - 8 =$ Wait a second. I have to take the flat away (regroup the 100 for

10 tens) so I would have 17 longs (tens), so $17 - 8 = 9$. So my answer is 92. Easy.

Cody's comment, "Easy," gives him the opportunity to show his confidence, an aspect that would be lost on a workbook page.

Joseph's journal revealed a personal mathematical interest, and it opened an avenue for further exploration:

$$310$$
$$- \underline{185}$$
$$125$$

In my head I know that two of my flats (100s) are gone (Joseph knows that the answer will be about 100) because it says to take one flat away and I have one long (a 10), but I need to take eight longs away. I have to take the flat away and get ten longs. Then I have to take eight longs away so I have two longs left. In my head I know that my number is going to be odd because a half of ten is five.

In addition to being very capable with mental computation, Joseph was obviously interested in odd and even numbers. Throughout the year, he continued to notice patterns of odd and even numbers in many contexts. I capitalized upon opportunities to encourage him to pursue this interest. If his work had been limited to a numerical answer, I might not have known about his interest in the odd-even property. Moreover, it is possible that Joseph himself may not have noticed the odd-even pattern in his computation without taking the time to write. Perhaps writing slowed him down, giving him time to reflect upon this mathematical relationship. In any case, this journal writing opened new potential for further investigations. Computation can lead to explorations of numerical patterns and relationships.

Mathematical Writing as a Tool for Discovery

I also apply lessons about reflection that I learned from Donald Murray and my middle-school students in this mathematical context. After writing about a mathematical investigation about any topic (computation, geometry, statistics, and so forth), I ask children, "Put your hand up if you thought of a new idea as you wrote and drew." A fair number of students always raise their hands, and we hold class discussions about the ways writing, drawing, and talking help us grow as mathematicians. I also ask the children to write about a classmate's strategy or insight that helped them that day so that we publicly acknowledge the social roots of our thinking. On other occasions I ask the children to sketch and write about the processes of talking, writing, and drawing in math class. As always, their comments aid me in reflecting about my teaching and learning. Jenna, for example, wrote about the generative nature of writing in her journal:

> When I write [in math] I get more ideas. See I know what I'm going to write, but by the time I get to a part, I get a new idea.

Sharing journals was also important to Bobby:

> We all get ideas off of each other. (His accompanying picture showed a classmate, Tony, saying, "We can trade the flat for ten longs." On the other side of the page Billy drew himself saying, "I got my idea off Tony.")

Starr's reflection acknowledged her confidence in building understanding of mathematical ideas:

> [Writing and drawing] teaches me how to learn. When I write I get lots of ideas of what else I want to say. It helps me learn how to draw and how to talk about math more. I can get ideas off of other people's papers and what they say would be clear.

Conclusion

These children's reflections show me so plainly much of what was missing in my earlier teaching, and I think they can help all of us on our teaching journeys. Jenna implies that writing helps generate ideas, no matter if the subject is math, science, or language. Her insight is a reminder to teachers that we need to examine common processes of thinking across subject areas. Bobby's reflection demonstrates that learners don't operate in isolation. Teachers, too, grow best in the company of others through conferences, workshops, study groups, reading, and informal visits "across the hall." Our friends, colleagues, and mentors help us view our teaching from fresh perspectives. Starr celebrates writing, talking, and drawing as tools for discovery. Teachers also need to write, talk, and draw in order to discover insights, make connections, and plan next steps. In these ways we can follow children's leads in continuing to grow as professional learners.

For the Instructional Conversation

In-Class or In-Group Thinking, Writing, and Talking

1. Review Phyllis' ideas on missed potential on the first page of her section. Here she introduces her thinking with a focus on writing prod-

ucts rather than processes. On your own skim her section and locate several instances in which Phyllis focuses on math and writing processes. Consider her teaching and your ideas about process-product instruction. Then share your ideas with a partner and pull your ideas together. Develop a short list of your ideas. Share with the entire class or group.

2. Review the Tharp and his co-authors' principles in Chapter 1; then review Phyllis' section, "Research, Writing, and Scientific Learning with Fourth-Graders." Brainstorm with the class or group on the ways in which you think Phyllis' teaching draws on these principles. Refine your thinking through small-group or partner work and note your ideas in writing. Support your findings with quotes from Phyllis or her students. Engage in large-group discussion and reach some consensus.

3. Review Phyllis' section and note instances of interactions among students (formulating ideas as well as publishing). Examine ways that Phyllis provided opportunities for children to collaborate, and discuss additional strategies from your own experience. Share your expanded list with the group.

Reflection for Thinking and Action

1. This is an activity that may be done now or later as you complete this book. Locate the section or chapter in which Doris (1991), *Doing What Scientists Do,* discusses building a respectful community. Then read about the classrooms of JoAnn Archie, Andrew Allen, and John Greenwell in Chapter 5. In a short paper or a power-point presentation, compare and contrast the more salient features of all four discussions. Draw conclusions about the teachers' and Doris' philosophies. Present your findings in class or in a group.

2. Select at least three math-related children's books recommended by Phyllis. Develop a lesson plan at your preferred grade level that provides for math instruction, reading and using one of the books, writing, and teacher-student discussion. Review your plans and write a short list of concerns you may have about it and its strengths. Share your plans with a math teacher or a peer. Ask for any concerns they may have about it and what they consider to be its strengths. Prepare to discuss your lesson plan. How did the writing and questioning of it with another person help or hinder you?

3. Design a math experience for children (of your preferred grade level) and plan for oral and written responses, drawing upon some of the open-ended prompts suggested in this section. Implement your plan

with a group of children or in a peer teaching experience. Reflect upon the kinds of observations learners make and the individuality of each student's voice. Write up a brief overview of your lesson and your reflections in a letter addressed to a teaching friend.

Chapter Summary

Both Kris and Phyllis developed an interest in mathematics from childhood experiences that were opposite in their negative and positive impact. Kris was hurt because of the rote learning, in one prescribed way to "to get answers" to problems for which she had no conceptual base. And Phyllis happily engaged in functional math in the grocery store play area her teacher provided. Thus, two different but deeply personal experiences brought two different human beings into the world of math and science teaching. One of the most striking elements of Kris' and Phyllis' math instruction is their focus on making math problems and processes authentic. From Valentine's card exchanges to using math with children's literature, both classrooms provide unique scaffolding for bringing math and science into the realm of everyday lives of children. Similarly, both teachers emphasize children's thinking in ways that draws them into a conceptual world of exciting ideas with no skill left untaught or unpracticed. The instruction in this chapter—as in the other chapters—demonstrates the work and responsibility of professional development, the joy of teaching in keeping with deeply held ideals, and the power of teachers' finding their own strengths and interests.

References

Appelt, K. 1996. *Bat Jamboree*. New York: Morrow.

Ayers, W. 1993. *To Teach*. New York: Teachers College Press.

Barnes, D. 1992. *From Communication to Curriculum*. 2d ed. Portsmouth, N.H.: Boynton/Cook.

Bird, L., K. S. Goodman, & Y. M. Boodman. 1994. *The Whole Language Catalog: Forms for Authentic Assessment*. New York: MacMillan/McGraw-Hill, SRA Division.

Borasi, R. 1992. *Learning Mathematics through Inquiry*. Portsmouth, N.H.: Heinemann.

Brown, M. W. 1990. *Four Fur Feet*. Columbia, Ala.: Hopscotch Books.

Cherry, L. 1990. *The Great Kapok Tree*. New York: Harcourt Brace.

Clement, R. 1991. *Counting on Frank*. Milwaukee: Gareth Stevens Children's Books.

Cole, J. 1985. *Large as Life Animals.* New York: Knopf.

Demi. 1997. *One Grain of Rice.* New York: Scholastic.

Doris, E. 1991. *Doing What Scientists Do.* Portsmouth, N.H.: Heinemann.

Facklan, M. 1994. *The Big Bug Book.* Boston: Little.

Gipson, F. 1956. *Old Yeller.* New York: Harper.

Graves, D. 1983. *Writing, Teachers and Children at Work.* Portsmouth, N.H.: Heinemann.

Harste, J., K. Short, & C. Burke. 1996. *Creating Classrooms for Authors and Inquirers.* Portsmouth, N.H.: Heinemann.

Harvey, S. 1998. *Nonfiction Matters.* York, ME: Stenhouse.

Heibert, J. 1997. *Making Sense: Teaching and Learning Mathematics with Understanding.* Portsmouth, N.H.: Heinemann.

Hoban, T. 1998. *So Many Circles, So Many Squares.* New York: Greenwillow.

Hulme, J. 1993. *Sea Squares.* New York: Hyperion.

Murray, D. 1967. *A Writer Teaches Writing.* Boston: Houghton.

Paulos, John Allen. 2000. *Innumeracy: Mathematical Illiteracy and Its Consequences.* London: Penguin.

Pinczes, E. 1995. *A Remainder of One.* Boston: HM.

Purcell-Gates, V. 1995. *Other People's Words: The Cycle of Low Literacy.* Cambridge, MA: HUP.

Schmitt, L. 1989. *Smart Spending: A Young Consumer's Guide.* New York: Scribners.

Schwartz, D. 1985. *How Much is a Million?* New York: Lothrop.

———. 1999. *If You Hopped Like a Frog.* New York: Scholastic.

Short, K., & J. Harste. 1996. *Creating Classrooms for Authors and Inquirers.* Portsmouth, N.H.: Heinemann.

Short, K., & K. Mercy. 1990. *Talking About Books: Creating Literate Communities.* Portsmouth, N.H.: Heinemann.

Tharp, R., P. Estrada, S. S. Dalton, & L. A. Yamauchi. 2001. *Teaching Transformed.* Boulder, CO: Westview Press.

Tyrell, E. 1985. *Hummingbirds, Their Life and Behavior, A Phtotgraphic Study of the North American Species.* New York: Crown.

———. 1986. *Hummingbirds: Jewels of the Sky.* New York: Crown.

White, E. B. 1970. *The Trumpet of the Swan.* New York: Harper.

Whitin, D. J. 1992. *Read Any Good Math Lately? Children's Books for Mathematical Learning K–6.* Portsmouth, N.H.: Heinemann.

Whitin, P., & D. Whitin. 1997. *Inquiry at the Window: Pursuing the Wonders of Learners*. Portsmouth, N.H.: Heinemann.

———. 2000. *Math is Language Too: Talking and Writing in the Mathematics Classroom*. Urbana, Ill.: National Council of Teachers of English, and Reston, Va.: National Council of Teachers of Mathematics.

Whitin, P., & S. Wilde. 1996. *Sketching Stories, Stretching Minds: Responding Visually to Literature*. Portsmouth, N.H.: Heinemann.

Yashima, T. 1986. *Hummingbirds: Jewels in the Sky*. New York: Crown.

———. 1955. *Crow Boy*. New York: Viking.

5

Building Community and Teaching With Respect

WITH CONTRIBUTIONS BY JOANN ARCHIE, ANDREW ALLEN, AND JOHN GREENWELL

Effective teaching is focused on developing classroom communities and building curriculum. These things are extremely important, because they make good skill and strategy instruction possible. Without a respectful, well-managed classroom, school becomes a place in which children *and* teachers fail to thrive.

It's important to draw distinctions between the concepts of discipline and control and those of creating a healthy classroom community. Thinking in terms of *discipline* and *control* puts well-intended teachers at a disadvantage. Maintaining a classroom in which children follow only the teacher's directions (which are usually dictated by the curriculum) and are not able to speak except when spoken to cannot be accomplished without more and more energy being spent on discipline. It is emotionally draining for teachers to reprimand students constantly and it is degrading for children. Although there must be classroom order and structure, a learning community can't exist under authoritarian control.

A caring and respectful classroom necessitates a sense of community, a place in which all participants belong and are treated as caring, responsible, and respected people. Children or teachers who are controlled and disciplined in the traditional sense are not part of an effective learning community. Because we know more about learning itself and the social and cognitive activities that support it, learning places (classrooms) in today's world do not look like the quiet, orderly places of a bygone era. Instead, well-managed classrooms feature children and teachers talking together, moving about the classroom with purpose, and acting together to direct their work. Well-managed action (and lots of it!) by individuals, small groups, and the whole class is a hallmark of an effective learning community.

The teachers featured in this chapter, JoAnn Archie, Andrew Allen, and John Greenwell, made choices about the kind of classroom in which they would teach. They knew the kind of effective classroom they had to manage in order to support professional, personal, and pedagogical development. Their focused goals include the following.

- to provide varied reading and writing materials and a range of genre embedded in high quality children's literature
- to provide children with varied and flexible ways in which they can engage with reading, writing, and studying
- to respect group and individual responses to reading materials
- to create ways in which they work with peers and in small groups
- to maintain a clear emphasis on "kid watching" (Goodman 1978) and shape teaching according to children's responses
- to work at making the learning environment feel like a safe place to take risks
- to teach children how to self-select wisely and how to self-assess as much as possible
- to teach explicitly and implicitly the behaviors that are acceptable in this classroom and those that are not by verbalizing your thinking, pointing out examples, and inviting the children to participate in creating their learning community
- to show that teachers are highly responsible people and that children are also responsible people
- to emphasize respect for the whole class and unique individual differences by creating student self-assessment, providing opportunities for student self-selection and input, and thus supporting their ownership of learning tasks.

These goals can be met by combining expert teacher guidance and intervention to help children move toward independent learning. Literate environments are safe places in which students can take risks in trying reading, writing, and voicing their views without fear or shame. In such classrooms children persist in learning through mistakes and successes. It is in this process that they acquire a "disposition for learning" (Dahl and Freppon 1995; Freppon 1995).

JoAnn Archie

JoAnn Archie: *Learning to Teach with Respect*

JoAnn Archie teaches in an inner-city school in Louisville, Kentucky. She has strong views on the importance of the social cohesiveness within a group and the significance of cultural awareness. She believes these factors impact in major ways on students' learning. Her teaching goals are to create community, respect, and self-discipline in her students.

Learning to Teach with Respect

In Chapter 1 you read about me and the principal who took new teachers to visit their students' neighborhoods. There we saw the world of experiences the children would bring into the classroom. I also noted that I learned that both the students and the teacher could have a hand in their own learning and that I held the belief that there was a humane way to teach.

During my first years of teaching I came to understand how the beliefs I held about children meshed with theory and research-based practice that I was learning through my professional development. I took literacy courses at the university, a Bill Martin workshop, a Reading Recovery workshop, and more workshops. I read several books on my own, including Routman's (1987) *Invitations,* Hansen's (1987) *When Writers Read,* Calkins' (1990) *Reading Between the Lines,* Fisher's (1991) *Joyful Learning,* and Strickland and Morrow's (1989) *Young Children Learn to Read and Write.* In addition, my principal informed me that there were a few whole language teachers in the building, and she suggested that I investigate their classrooms to find out what they knew about helping children become literate that I didn't already know. I began to observe them in their classrooms. At the time I didn't have a clearly defined teaching philosophy. I just knew that I wanted to be a good teacher and that a way to achieve this goal was to take classes and observe expert teachers. I attempted to apply both the theory and research-based strategies in my own classroom. Through this experimental period I came to understand that my goals for achieving a sense of community fit philosophically with my goals for literacy instruction.

For example, in my university courses I learned that children need good writing models and that they need to own the writing process and products (their stories are theirs, not mine!). From watching my colleagues I learned that I too needed models. How wise my principal had been to advise me to observe. I realized that I had to own my own teaching process—that I had to make sense of the experts' ideas by blending them with my own. I had to and I have to continually revise what I am doing to make sure my students' needs are being met. Using a model and trying it out, watching the students, revising instruction, and owning it became the process I used for building community and literacy instruction in my classroom. For me, *owning it* means that theory-based instruction must resonate with my philosophy and beliefs. Here are some descriptions of the ways in which this occurs in my classroom.

Building Community Is the Heart of Classroom Management

Teaching and learning happen best when individuals in the classroom feel comfortable with who they are—i.e., when students have a sense of belonging and feel accepted and respected, they learn better. Unless conscious efforts are made to build camaraderie or a sense of community, all other teacher "know-how" is futile. Effective classrooms do not just appear; they are built. Children will not feel safe if they do not feel comfortable with the cultures, appearances, or experiences they bring to the classroom. Feelings of difference may inhibit a child's willingness to take risks, and risk-taking is an essential part of an effective learning environment. In addition, students must care not only about their own achievements but also about their classmates' achievements (Ladson-Billings 1994, 69).

Holistic Instruction as a Foundation for Building Community

Early on, I learned two important lessons with the help of a sensitive and wise first principal (the one who took all of us on field trips to the children's neighborhoods).

- In order to best teach students, we must know them, who they are, where they come from, and how they live.

- We must respect each child and accept what each one brings to the classroom community.

As Moll and González (1994) have shown us, we must build on the experiences and strengths the students bring. My techniques for classroom community building, instruction, and management stand on the shoulders of university course work, conferences I attend, on theory I've been taught, and on my own readings of Regie Routman, Dorothy Strickland, Bill Martin, and others. An old proverb, "Highlight my strengths and my weaknesses will disappear," challenges and supports me. I try to use this mantra when examining children's writing and helping them improve. But I also use it to apply to children's backgrounds, behaviors, and language. Here are some of the things I do in order to meet my teaching goals.

- I shun methods of keeping track of student's failings, such as "assertive discipline." Writing the child's name on the board and saying "Your name is up! That's a check! That's another check!" is demeaning and unproductive.
- I avoid looking at the negative and claiming "There is little we can do—look at what they (children) go through at home."

In contrast to things I don't do, the following are ideas and guidelines that I find most helpful. As I work through these strategies, I can achieve the kind of community I wish for my students.

- Keep constantly in mind that I want students to think about their actions.
- Show children ways they can take responsibility for themselves.
- Focus on not telling children every wrong move they make (they will not learn to think for themselves in this environment).
- Highlight the positive, catch children doing wise and positive things, and point them out and discuss them with the whole class. (This takes much practice, for as teachers our culture traditionally stresses correcting and controlling.)

Strategies for Community Building: Respect, Effective Instruction, and a Well-managed Classroom

My previous school and the one where I now teach have high populations of at-risk children. The process of classroom community building and the establishment of rules are strongly influenced by what many refer to as the Golden Rule. Kindness and respect for all members of the community are stressed at all times. To this end, I use some of Ruth Charney's (1992) and Barbara Colorso's (1987) methods, which focus on valuing the child.

As much as my children want to behave appropriately, *they simply do not always know what is inappropriate.* They need clearly defined rules as a reference for their misbehavior. And they need to talk about our standards of behavior. Talking with the child about the behavior and hearing his or her side shows respect for the child while admonishing the behavior.

Every year of my teaching career I have to rethink my approach to classroom rules. Children need clearly defined rules as a reference. They need to talk about behavior and they often need to talk about it many times early in the year. With the children, I develop a small set of classroom rules (three to five is a good number), with the Golden Rule governing all others. My primary-grade set of class rules include:

1. Treat others with kindness and respect.
2. Listen carefully when someone else is talking.
3. Follow directions.
4. Work quietly during quiet work time.

It's important to stress that it takes time to build the psychological safety that is crucial for a supportive community. For example, I am able to work efficiently with rule-breaking situations. I explicitly teach appropriate behavior and thinking by asking, "What is another way you could have handled this?" This kind of teacher response must be learned by the teacher and taught to the children. We cannot assume children know how to return to a peaceful state when things around them have been in chaos.

Community respect, effective instruction, and a well-managed classroom are not created easily. At the beginning of each school year I am usually overwhelmed at how disruptive students are, how inappropriate their talk or laughter can be, and how disrespectful they can be without knowing it. I become exasperated until I remind myself that each new group of children needs time and instruction. This realization on my part, some simple rules, and respectful consequences for misbehavior help support classroom community building and thus my ability to teach well.

Students need consequences, but the consequences should not punish students by keeping them from the good things our classrooms have to offer. Every child has a right to the classroom's learning opportunities. Isolating children or sending the out of my room denies them opportunities to learn. To manage my classroom well, I know that children must realize that they are respected, even as their behavior has consequences when they make an inappropriate choice.

As noted previously, one of our rules is Listen carefully when someone else is talking. I call attention to this idea by reading it and having children discuss it. I explain that listening means hearing what I have to say. I say to the children, "To really hear someone, you can't be thinking about what you are going to say, so no hands should be raised while someone else is talking." Explaining this once, of course, is certainly not enough. I have to demonstrate or explain, patiently and gently several times a day for weeks, exactly how to listen before students begin to truly listen to each other. Their skill at doing this gets better over the course of the school year.

Once the class works through learning the few rules noted previously, I use some easy and respectful consequences to help them learn to manage their own behavior. For example, I raise my eyebrows, utter a low, firm "Take care of it," and send the child off to write the rule that has been broken and an explanation about why it was broken and a plan to change behavior. Initial pleas such as "But . . . I" are stopped until the child has written the rule and the explanation. When children reflect upon inappropriate behaviors and plan for more appropriate ways to interact within the community, the outcomes are of greater magnitude. This approach allows the student to be in charge of his or her failures and successes.

This technique gives the child time to calm down and practice writing explanatory text and gives me time to get to the child to deal with the issue. This practice seems to prevent a lot of little problems that can be avoided because children know that breaking a rule leads to some hard thinking about behavior. Notice that this kind of behavior intervention puts the child in a responsible position. Each one is in charge of addressing the consequences of behavior that is inappropriate in our classroom.

As much as individual student responsibility is critical to instruction and managing the classroom, children also need to develop a sense of cooperation and their relationship to the whole community. Teaching this concept also requires demonstration and discussion. One example of a technique that works well for me is making a whole-class jigsaw puzzle, which can be done in a few easy steps.

- I draw a freehand design and make a puzzle that is easily cut into pieces—one for each child.
- The children decorate their pieces and come to me in small groups to fit the puzzle together.
- When the puzzle is finished, we have a collage of children's artwork in which each piece relies on the others to make the whole.
- We talk about the interacting pieces of our puzzle and about the importance of each piece in making the whole complete.

Explicit Instruction for Children's Self-Management

Explicit instruction is usually thought about in terms of teaching literacy strategies and skills. Lisa Delpit (1995) has helped me and countless other educators think better and harder about how we teach reading and writing explicitly. The importance of explicit instruction cannot be overstated. All children need it sometimes, and some children need it nearly all the time. Yet, it is also true that this way of teaching is applicable to classroom management and community and curricula building. I learned this truth by watching my students. The following event with Charles Adams helps illustrate how I learned that children need explicit modeling and demonstration to learn how to manage their classroom behavior.

After some inappropriate behavior, I asked Charles, "What is another way you could have handled this?" He responded with a blank look. Then I realized that social skills must be directly and explicitly modeled and explained every bit as much as literacy skills. Based on this insight, I have some strategies on which I rely to get children's attention and to make daily transitions run smoothly.

- Stand quietly and count under your breath. Students soon notice and watch.

- When all is quiet, explain, "When I am upset about your behavior I will not scream at you. Instead I count because it makes me calm down."

- Repeat—and repeat—the teaching of all components of building classroom community (e.g., respectful rules and consequences) and actual assignments.

- Demonstrate regularly how to do the simple things, such as moving chairs quietly, and complex things, such as using learning centers.

- Initiate a clapping or finger-snapping pattern to get children's attention. As they hear the pattern, they join in until all members are clapping or snapping. Then stop and expect all children to look toward the teacher for the message.

I also count by twos the number of eyes I see looking at me.

Children often find this a puzzle at first and enjoy trying to figure out what I am doing. When I get to 48 (for 24 children), for example, I am ready to speak to the class.

Another effective strategy is using classical music to soothe or help the class think; for instance, I play a tape recording of soft classical music during writing time. This seems to communicate that quiet is expected and that this is a time for peaceful work. A different tape (a song with lyrics) might indicate when it is time to put materials away and get ready for lunch.

The concrete cueing of music and my structure for using it speaks explicitly about what children are to do and how they need to do it. The children use soft voices when the music is on. In some tasks they work in time to the music.

In the past I used to just nag the children: "Please put the materials away. Clear your desk. Line up to wash your hands." This always dragged on far longer than it should, and it exasperated me. Through my own graduate study and a fortunate observation of an outstanding local teacher, I learned how to use music. Now, when the children are working in the learning centers and it is close to time for lunch, I put on a tape of "Lean on Me" or another song. The children know this is a signal to put materials away, wash their hands, and line up at the door before the song is over. There is usually a mass rush during the final stanza, but this simple, pleasant routine eliminates the nagging that so often goes into making transitions with young children. During the songs, many often dance a little to the music as they sing and put materials away. Allowing them to move acknowledges children's desire to feel the rhythm of the music. It shows my respect for them. And I can see the relaxed sense of belonging on their faces.

In all the techniques I've discussed, I model the behavior and explicitly tell children why I choose to react as I do and what I expect them to do. (This kind of teaching is referred to as *skills streaming* by McGinnis and Goldstein (1997)). Eventually, however, explicit behavior instruction is no longer necessary. By midyear, I can gain students' attention in a matter of seconds, and they can make reasonably smooth transitions independently.

Get Real: Authentic Self and Curriculum

Early in my teaching career I received a lot of advice from well-meaning colleagues. One was to give an opening-day speech. It was a script that told me what to say to the children on the first day about how they should behave (complete with facial expressions)! It was intended to communicate that I mean business. I decided to give it a try. There I was, a person who finds laughter to be the best medicine for the inner being, trying to maintain a grim stance before these precious little ones. It was very unnatural for me to follow this guide, and I quickly evolved into the real me before the students' eyes. Following "manufactured" teacher-student interaction limits the meaningfulness of the relationships that can be built in the classrooms. It's best to keep interactions genuine, with consideration of the fact that, in general, all humans like being treated honestly and with care.

Teachers need to show children that everyone makes mistakes. Classroom communities in which children feel safe are places in which they feel like talking about their own errors and (on rare occasion!) those of the teacher. These healthy responses are built by example upon honest example.

Personal and Professional Journeys Take Time and Attention

Unsure of what children should be doing and learning, I have used my share of worksheets and textbooks. But, children are bored by assignments that do not relate to their lives. Developing authentic curriculum is an ongoing challenge for every teacher. I find I can connect with student's lives fairly easily through children's literature.

I use books by and about African Americans, such as *Honey, I Love* by Eloise Greenfield (1978), and about rural whites, such as *When I Was Young in the Mountains* by Cynthia Rylant (1985). We also read books that make us believe in ourselves, books that teach us to accept one another, such as *Roop and Roop* (1985), *Keep the Lights Burning*, Steptoe (1996), *Mufaro's Beautiful Daughters*, and Mitchell (1997) *Uncle Jed's Barbershop*. Literature in the classroom relates to my students' lives in teaching reading, writing, mathematics, history, and science. Good books link literate language and the content to children's experiences, as the following example shows.

Following a reading of *Nathaniel Talking* by Greenfield (1988), a book written in rap,

- I transcribed part of the text onto a chart for the students to read.
- After reading and enjoying the words for awhile, the children performed various lines.
- We discussed the meanings of some of the words, particularly the word *philosophy*, which is a prominent word in the book.
- Finally, I invited some children to share their personal philosophies.

This particular lesson occurred after studying the Civil Rights movement, and a child said, "I think all people are equal." Another said, "Everyone should get to go to the school they want to go to." I also shared some of my own philosophies (about teaching, of course), such as "Children should get to choose what they want to read on most days." I ended this lesson by showing spelling and phonics patterns and putting new words (from our reading) on our word family chart. In an effort to connect closely to children's participation styles and learning preferences, I vary activities to include individual and cooperative work, discovery time, and time for talking to help children learn concepts.

Building on what students know is a way that also shows respect for the learners. Showing respect for students encompasses more than human kindness and extends into curricular methods and expectations as I have shown. Showing respect does not mean "babying" children. Showing respect means having high expectations and providing opportunities for high-level thinking. I demand that my students not only give answers but also reasons for their answers. I ask questions such as

- Why? How do you know that?
- Can you explain how you got that answer?
- Explain your thinking.

At first, children think if they have to explain their answers that their thinking must be wrong. But they soon learn that they have reasons for their answers and that they must learn to articulate them. This kind of high-level thinking shows respect for the students' minds, and in turn, helps them respect themselves.

As every good teacher knows, hard work and high expectations are important in creating a classroom community. Students know when you truly care.

I remember a day when I was having a writing conference with a child. He was sharing his narrative from his writer's notebook, and we were struggling through his spelling and organization problems. After a while, he looked up at me and said, "You know, we are kind of like a family." I smiled and said, "You know, I think you're right." It is at these moments when it all seems worth the work and I am motivated to press forward.

Teaching Responsibility: School Is for Them

I have a sign in my classroom that reads, "Who is doing the thinking in this classroom?" A professor reminded me a few years ago that if I am doing more of the thinking in my classroom than my students, I am defeating myself as a teacher. I liked his philosophy because it fit with my own about creating classroom community. I believe that students must do the majority of the thinking and decision-making in the classroom; they must learn to be responsible for their learning and their behavior. Coming to this understanding was not easy, and my work on understanding continues today.

With each new class I *work* on helping children take responsibility for their behavior, for our classroom, and for their learning. Early in the year, when I am focused on teaching children responsibility, I'll ask children to role-play a skill or one of our class rules. Then as situations arise, students can "rewind" situations so they can act out in a more appropriate way to solve their own problems. A few benchmark-teaching moves on my part go a long way:

- Asking the students, "Can you think of a better way to solve this problem?" can help students back up and rethink their behaviors.
- Holding small-group meetings with those involved in a conflict and sometimes having them reenact the situation with a different solution that yields a different ending is helpful.

The following vignette illustrates how these discussions unfold in the classroom.

> A little girl was observed snatching glue during a group project, which resulted in a tug-of-war with another child. I strategically became visible to the children but just stood by and watched. When they finally looked up at me, I asked them, "What's another way?" The glue-snatcher offered, "I could pour some glue on the paper and then give the bottle back."

In my time of more traditional teaching, I would have told this child what to do. But now, allowing her to think of the solution scaffolds her ability to take responsibility. My response demonstrates a sense of trust in her ability to think. To focus my behavior in this way I hold onto the idea of "Ask, don't tell."

In one-to-one scaffolding, I try to get children to assume responsibility for their academic learning as well as behavior. For example, I was reading with LaMonte one day, and he stumbled on the word *aphids*. He tried to sound it out.

Sometimes p-h makes the /fff/ sound, I told him.

He read, A-phids.

Then I asked him, What are aphids?

LaMonte shrugged, and I said, Read the rest of the sentence. Then think about what aphids could be.

LaMonte read the rest of the sentence and then asked, "Like, bugs?"

I nodded. He read on. He came to the word *suggested*. He decoded it as best he could.

I asked him, Now what can you do?

Read on?

Yes.

LaMonte read on and again figured out the word.

Use that word in another sentence, I said, to be sure.

My mom suggested that I . . . he began.

After reading a paragraph, I turned to him and said, Go back and reread the paragraph so you can think about what you read. That's what good readers do.

Beyond trying to get students to assume responsibility for figuring out words on their own, I point out what they need to do and why. My goal is to get students such as LaMonte to read texts of their choice independently.

Sing! Dance! Act! Use the Arts for Community Building

My students love music and respond positively to its use for a variety of purposes. Sometimes we just turn on music and sing songs that inspire me to keep teaching and keep believing, such as the one I learned at the Bill Martin workshop: "I like you. You like me and I am Freedom's child." We also enjoy "When Love Comes Back to You," and a favorite is "Lean On Me," which some of the children sing loudly while playing pretend guitars or using pretend microphones. We learn from these songs that we need different kinds of people in the world. Singing makes us feel good, and feeling good is essential for a sense of pride, learning, and belonging in the classroom community.

Using drama is also an inspiring way for children to learn literacy skills and a healthy self-esteem. I try to work drama into everyday lessons and have a full-scale class play each year. Here is how one of our classroom sessions worked.

- I read poems from Eloise Greenfield's (1978), *Honey, I Love.*
- The children listened closely to the first poem in the book, and we discussed it and enjoyed the language.
- I had written each poem stanza on individual index cards.
- In pairs (or small groups) the children were to practice and perform their stanza to clean up miscues in their reading and become fluent with the text.

- After practicing and getting ready for the performance, the children added the snapping of their fingers and a rap rhythm (a common product in this classroom).

The children were so proud of themselves that they clapped and laughed afterwards, praising one another. This lesson was an easy way to: (1) respect children's learning styles and interests, (2) make reading authentic through purpose and sense of audience, and (3) build intrinsic motivation (Oldfather and West 1999) to improve children's reading and oral language skills.

For our class play one year, we used the book *The Josephina Story Quilt* (Coerr 1986), complete with our own script, costumes and three-dimensional displays about the westward movement. This occurred after the students compared the traditional European American account with Brenner's (1993) *Wagon Wheels*, an account of an African American family making the westward movement.

Keeping Your Head Up

Creating a classroom community is not easy. There were—and still are—moments that devastate me. For instance, after discussing treating others as you want to be treated, I once saw someone in our community strike another group member. This, after we had just sat and exchanged our deep feelings about the necessity of respect. The incident was so discouraging. It was—and still is—at these moments that I question the effectiveness of my work in building classroom community. It is at these times that it seems the very foundation of my philosophy begins to crumble. Even today there are times when I leave the school for the day questioning my abilities as a teacher.

In spite of efforts to convince myself that perhaps I should turn to a more authoritarian method of teaching and outlining daily regimens with no student input, something within the community will say to my inner being, "Hold on to what you know. The end results will be far better." And so, I continue my work and use the struggle to become stronger. In these ways I continue to reap the joys of teaching.

I think back on that first year when I visited the neighborhoods of the children I would teach. Yes, they were poor, and there were some unexpected items on the porches and in the back yards. However, there was also a family member in many of the residences who seemed eager for the child to succeed in school. Too often as teachers we see the negative when we could be highlighting the positive. Too often I hear teachers say there is little they can do for diverse children with low-income backgrounds. If I am not watchful I find myself being drawn into this belief system—after all it does allow me to escape my own feelings of inadequacy. However, upon brief consideration, my personal and philosophical beliefs keep me grounded.

As I watch my students grow into respectful people who strive to learn, I am reminded that I belong here and of why I chose to do this work in the first place. How does it feel to work on learning to teach? It becomes so worthwhile.

For the Instructional Conversation

In-Class or In-Group Thinking and Action

1. The preface of this book lists its purposes. One purpose is to show the value of teacher inquiry and the necessity of research-based teaching to provide access to effective instruction and classroom management. Use this point as a guide to selecting passages from JoAnn's section that demonstrate her teaching and classroom management through the instructional conversation with children or with a child. Jot down these passages and your insights so you can use your notes to talk with others.

2. Examine the list of Ayers' attributes of exemplary teaching in Chapter 1. In small groups or with a partner, find evidence of as many of these characteristics as you can in JoAnn's piece. List them individually or jointly and compare the list with another. Is there any negative evidence? Can you create a negative or another positive piece of evidence?

3. JoAnn works both on creating community and on effective instruction. Do you think that these teaching goals are mutually inclusive or goals that can be in conflict? Develop a list on each side of the topic and push yourself to examine these questions critically. Discuss your ideas.

Reflective Thinking and Action

1. JoAnn used some of her professors' or other mentors' ideas to create words of wisdom such as, "Who is doing the learning in this classroom?" to guide her teaching. Ask some professors or teachers you admire about their teaching, learning, or theoretical "nuggets." Polish those nuggets by thinking about what they have said and respond to it. To extend your thinking, create a short vignette, a drawing, or other representation, such as a scene from a play, in which the power of one of these ideas may be shown in process.

2. JoAnn refers to Gloria Ladson-Billings (1994) book, *The Dreamkeepers: Successful Teachers of African American Children,* several times. Read this book or any other like-minded book and prepare an informal narrative that you might use to help a new teacher to better understand children such as those JoAnn teaches. To elaborate, try this narrative out on someone (a new teacher if at all possible) and capture her or his responses.

3. Make a list of the thoughts and actions that JoAnn uses to help create community. Interview 2–4 teachers who see themselves, and are seen by others, as good classroom community builders. Generate a list of each teacher's interview responses that show his/her thought and action in building community. Compare and construct lists and discuss them with others.

Andrew Allen: *A Democratic Literature-Based Curriculum*

At age eighteen Andrew emigrated from Jamaica. After his degree in mechanical engineering technology, Andrew began volunteering in schools and found he loved working there. The rest is history. Andrew Allen taught second grade in an urban school in Toronto, Canada. The school has more than 700 students and is situated in a dense urban area very much like Jack George's in the eastern United States. The students are from a very diverse cultural background with high immigration and migration and underemployed families.

Andrew Allen

I began teacher education wanting my future students to acquire the breadth, self-esteem, and satisfaction that come with being literate. I wanted them to know good books, to be able to use them throughout their lives for work and pleasure and in their relationships with others. Beyond learning to read and write, school must prepare children for life and for living literate lives.

Thus, I easily bonded with the notion of good books for my students. Whole language and constructivist-based philosophy emphasizes teaching with children's literature. Moreover, I liked the way this philosophy connects the students to one another, the teacher, the school, and the curriculum. I saw and still see this philosophy as a strong support in building a multicultural, antiracist, and antibias curriculum that addresses social justice. I saw and still see this philosophy as democratic (see Edelsky, 1994).

As indicated in Chapter 1 I was not a happy young student. In my own schooling, I read texts that had little or no meaning for me. And I certainly had no choice about what I read. In addition, because of the authoritarian stance of my teachers, I was embarrassed and sometimes shamed. An experience such as this can destroy a child's desire to learn and can damage self-esteem for life. I identify with the words of one of my favorite writers, Max Van Manen (1996), who warns that it may take some children the rest of their lives to understand the disarray of their school memories. As strange as it may seem, however, I lost sight of my negative experiences and some of my beliefs as I began to teach. In this trying period I do not believe that I was an authoritarian teacher who caused my students shame. But, I did cause them to feel uncomfortable and perhaps embarrassed for a while. This happened because in the beginning I attended to more surface-level aspects of my philosophy, such as (just) using multicultural books. I had not yet sufficiently learned the deeper meanings of my beliefs. Bottom line, I was green.

Professional development is very personal for me; through it I've found how profoundly my past schooling and likely my being an immigrant influenced my early teaching. I don't think that either one of these issues is much different than those other teachers have dealt with. Even teachers with good school experiences and the benefits of being native in their culture have their own tensions and worries to overcome. We all learn to teach in practice.

Learning to Teach and Being a Newcomer

When I started teaching, I worked to cope with the constant pressures of appearing to be competent. I felt I had to "fit in." My first job was teaching second grade in a school that served low-income, diverse, urban students, and most of my colleagues ran a very tight ship. That meant the children were kept busy with tons of paperwork and teachers' lesson plans were exact. I know from reading the literature that beginning teachers often tend to teach the way we were taught (Britzman 1991). Still, I had the goal of teaching in ways that were consistent with my beliefs, and I so much wanted to create a democratic community in my classroom.

For some time, I worked extremely hard doing several things at once. That is, I tried to look good to other people and be true to my convictions. Importantly, as a Black teacher, I assumed that my use of multicultural literature would be successful from the start.

I brought multicultural books into my classroom, read them to my students, and used them to teach reading. I was baffled, however, when my students of African heritage generally avoided reading certain books or seemed to be uncomfortable when I read to them. I had behavior problems because the children were not comfortable—they were conflicted. This insight and others helped me change. It was through my inner dialogue, reading, and discussions in graduate school that I finally began to use classroom problems to learn rather than as something to justify scolding children and venting my own frustrations.

I got a wake-up call from observing my students. During one small-group reading lesson, for example, a child asked to be dismissed to go to the washroom. Soon, other students started asking to go to the washroom. Even on good days my second graders appeared to be uninterested; they fidgeted in their seats.

As I struggled to teach and maintain order, I realized that I was totally unaware of the *children's perceptions* of their curriculum and instruction. Importantly, I had not properly prepared them for dealing with the social issues that were so often part of the classroom literature. Worse, I blamed the children for their inattention, and I failed to provide them with self-selection opportunities.

Building a Multicultural Program: Getting Back on the Road to Building a Democratic Community

To respond constructively to students' behavior problems I questioned my power and privilege in the classroom and observed students closely. What children read and how they feel about what they read is critical to their learning to read and to their behavior. Moreover, school may also be their first contact with books (Kiefer 1983) and can be the most salient contact in their lives. I knew I had to get this right.

I began to ask my students to select the books they wanted to read from our classroom library as well as those they wanted me to read to them. More important, I asked them to talk about books they did not want to read. Here are some ways I worked with my second-graders (Allen 1996):

- Discuss picture book illustrations. This is particularly important for young children, who use illustrations a great deal in their understanding of the text.
- Don't assume that just because a book is multicultural, it will automatically appeal to all diverse students.
- Track the books students select and talk to them about how they feel about the books.

When I asked my students why they liked a book or did not like a book, they were very forthcoming, as the following exchange shows. A boy chose to read *Leo the Late Bloomer* (Kraus 1971), and he explained. "I read that one before (pointing to Leo) and books make you smarter." A peer handed a book to her classmate and recommended, "You could get interested [in it] if you read it." The book *Daniel's Dog* (Bogart 1990) was a favorite with many of the children. In another instance, a struggling reader said about *Daniel's Dog,* "I know this book. Our teacher read this to us. I'm reading this. It is the best. I read it at school before."

The main character in *Daniel's Dog* is an African American boy who has an imaginary dog. The realistic images portray a range of expressions in the characters, particularly the children. They show excitement and sadness while at play. The illustrations are brightly colored, and the background is filled with objects that reflect an urban environment familiar to my students.

When second-graders selected unfamiliar books, they examined the covers and looked at pictures and the titles before they decided to read them. In the beginning, they "read" the pictures to see what the story was about. Thus, the illustrations, color, and formatting and meaning carried in the images played a strong role in their perceptions.

Some students indicated they did not want to read books that portrayed characters in certain settings. For example, they said that the pictures in a book with an African jungle setting looked weird, ugly, and funny (odd to these children). One student refused to read a picture book that depicted scantily clad African characters living in a remote area. The background showed a Savannahlike area with shrubs, cattle, and grass huts. In another instance, a student said, "I don't want to read about it [slavery]—I just don't," in reference to the books *Galimoto* (Williams 1990) and *The Orphan Boy* (Mollel

1990). When I heard this, I immediately talked with the child. Without going into a long explanation about slavery or questioning him, I validated his response. I told this child there were things I didn't like to read sometimes because they made me mad or unhappy. I let him know that he could tell me about his feelings anytime and that I was glad he had spoken up this time.

None of these picture books are about slavery. However, these incidents with the children showed me that they perceived the poverty markers in the illustrations as an indication that the books would be about slavery, war, hardship or poverty. They told me they liked "funny stories" and "happy pictures."

As you can see, using multicultural literature is far more complex than simply getting these books into the classroom and curriculum. I found that my belief that I could provide specific learning opportunities by having certain types of books available to my students simply did not work. Fortunately, I found that what the children needed was a level of caring I had failed to provide. Many teachers and researchers validate that caring is a very important part of teaching well. This point seems so obvious that most of us don't question it. I certainly thought I was a caring teacher. Yet, Van Galen (1993) describes caring as not being caring unless those being cared for perceive it as caring. This concept of caring was one of the greatest lessons I had to learn before I could build an effective curriculum with children's literature. Other factors I find important in my instruction are these:

- acknowledging that I can get caught up in the tensions of managing the classroom and using specific literature and thus miss some truly important things that are occurring right before me
- knowing that effective teaching requires taking a step back, carefully analyzing what is happening, and applying a critical eye on one's instruction
- understanding children's rights to ownership and self-efficacy in the classroom (This is not an easy concept to firmly ground in everyday practice, but it is crucial.)

In my search for better teaching I structured new opportunities to help children engage deeply with books through talk and various peer and teacher-student activities. I worked to provide opportunities for my students to learn to express their own sense of fairness and justice. The following example illustrates how I accomplished a more effective use of multicultural children's literature. The example involves a book some children rejected when I simply said, "Here, read this." Used differently, this same text works very well.

The book *Galimoto* (William 1990) functions as part of a technology unit on how things work. The story is about a child in central Africa who uses discarded cans, wires, and cardboard to construct his own toy car. Here are some inquiry-based steps I took with this book.

- Set the stage by having students bring old electronic and mechanical toys or devices from home to class.
- Have children take these toys apart, talk about them, and figure out how they work.
- Ask children to record their discoveries and ideas in logbooks.
- Introduce *Galimoto,* have children make log entries as we read the book, and reread parts as we discuss it.
- Discuss the main character's ingenuity and resourcefulness.
- Talk about the author's intention in writing this book.
- Pick up on or introduce issues of poverty and social justice (the children taught me to do this because they usually brought up such topics in their own ways).

In preparation for reading *Galimoto,* I once took my class to a local science center to see a display of toys constructed out of garbage. In addition to having a good time together, visiting this exhibit helped make more authentic reading and writing connections.

I use another multicultural book, *The Orphan Boy* (Mollel 1990). This book is a Masai folktale and not necessarily a story about a child living in Africa. The images carried another story for my students, who saw the illustrations as a reflection of real life. Young children rely less on abstractions, metaphors, double meanings, flashbacks, etc. Here is a brief description of how I used this book.

- Show the book cover, which depicts an African child in an empty, open area with no familiar urban reference.
- Wait for children to think and respond to the unfamiliar environment and the child's lonely stance. (In this case they assumed that the story would not be of interest to them.) Prompt and support their responses.
- Talk with the children and establish our collective purpose for reading this book.
- Work on reading skills (an inviting way to teach word recognition with second-graders).

In this case, we decided that we were going to read this book not for entertainment, but to learn more about the author's account of what it was like in another country. For word work I listed children's ideas on words that were hard for them on chart paper, pointed out words in the book, talked about meanings, and discussed the words' letter and sound relationships.

Children wrote the words from this chart-paper list on their own paper. They talked about the words with a partner and with me. This provided practice with word recognition and an authentic writing experience. Writing is most useful when it is a tool for achieving a purpose (rather than a performance). This lesson also supported the development of the children's social-emotional intellect in learning about another person's homeland and way of life.

In the end the students concluded that they liked the book (the children's way of saying it had value). They thought that the author was offering an appropriate point of view about people living in that part of Africa. Compare the children's responses to this reading of *Orphan Boy* and to an earlier reading in which the children had no voice in why or how the book was to be read (sad teacher). In this second case the children had the opportunity to collaborate on their decisions, to read critically, to participate in more dialogue, and to use their skills in context. The instruction was more child-centered, more authentic—and more democratic (much happier teacher).

Daily Routines in a Democratic Classroom

Generally, I follow this pattern in my teaching:

- Create a literate environment that supports ownership, self-selection, and responsible behavior.
- While teaching reading, work with texts that depict socially relevant issues.
- Encourage children to locate and name social issues, such as poverty, in the literature.
- As a class, examine the poverty markers that represent particular regional or racial and ethnic groups.
- Question the literature by asking, Why are the characters dressed liked that? Why do you think they live this way?
- Read and talk about the authors of our books.

My class also discusses traditional images in the media. Through TV, in particular, they become very adept at showing how stereotypes develop through images of particular groups. We've even discussed what it might be like to have the access and privilege of commercial publishing. As a class, with my demonstrations, we research books and use the Internet to locate biographical information about authors and illustrators of children's literature.

We discuss the process of getting a story published by one of the publishing houses. I use the children's stories in our classroom publishing center to talk about how books get published. We explore whose story gets published and who decides on this. In our room, of course, everyone has equal access to publishing, but this discussion about the selection process and issues of privilege prompts thoughtful talk.

I also use as an example my perceptions and power in the classroom as the teacher. Even second-grade students can readily relate to teacher power and privilege! Young children can understand nearly any issue in our society when teachers work to create trusting classroom communities and work on caring and thoughtfulness. Teachers' enjoyment of their work is also an extremely important factor in effective teaching. Children know when this is the case and when it is not. In my program I aim not only to help children learn to read, but also to help them learn a love of reading (Cochrane, Cochrane, Scalena, and Buchannan 1984).

Guided book discussions are important to children's social-emotional and academic growth. Shannon (1992) reminds us that children's literature can serve as a tool to teach students to detect and critically analyze bias as they read. The usual inquiry methods work well in researching social justice, just as they do in science and math. For example:

- Children may use maps, webs, notes, and letters to examine and write about the point of view of the author, illustrator, and publisher.
- Children may write about story characters or search and separate classroom books by specific categories.
- Children may record and graph the country of manufacture of their clothing or shoes they wear. One year our class discovered that many sneakers were made in poorer countries, and so we discussed why it might be cheaper to manufacture goods in those places.

As I've grown and developed as a teacher, I have experienced tremendous growth as a person. I've learned to manage my classroom as an effective learning place and to achieve many of my goals. I believe that my students gain breadth as literate persons and that they know and like books. It is even possible that books will remain a part of their lives as I have hoped—in work and pleasure and in their relationships with others, they may have good books for life.

When I set about making multicultural literature work in my classroom, I never dreamed that young children could learn and respond to books the way my students have. I enabled this level of learning and literate response by the way I structured my teaching talk and action and, importantly, by paying close attention to the children. This kind of teaching has never become easy for me. But, I'm better at it now. I accomplish more planning and thinking in less time, and observing the children is nearly automatic. But my teaching always requires hard thinking and careful deliberation. In this realm I find exactly what I need as a person and a professional educator.

For the Instructional Conversation

In-Class or In-Group Thinking and Action

1. Andrew's personal and professional development is based on certain principles. Look back through his section and write a short piece involving some lines or words used to show his principles and some lines used to show that Andrew searched for or used his personal strengths to improve his teaching. Share with a partner or in a small group. Quickly write a few lines or words that show your own principles and personal strengths that are helping you or will help you grow and change in your teaching.

2. Consider your ideas on the issue of "fitting in" in a new teaching position. Draw on your imagined and actual experiences or those of a friend. Sketch or use a graphic organizer (map, web, or cluster) to demonstrate your thoughts. Exchange papers with someone and try to understand what this person's ideas are before you discuss them.

3. Select one of these questions and respond to them orally or in writing. Compare and contrast in class or in a group:
   - How should race, class, and gender be woven into the curriculum for primary-grade students? Write, discuss, and compare.
   - Race, class, and gender should not be woven into the curriculum for primary-grade students. Write, discuss, and compare.
   - How should teachers deal with sociocultural differences in their classrooms?
   - How do you or how would you work with children who are different from you?

Reflective Thinking and Action

1. Ask three or more practicing teachers to name the most popular books in their classrooms. Ask the teachers why they think the children choose these books. Visit these classrooms during a discussion period and ask

the children to talk about their favorite books. Compare your responses with a colleague and generate a list of similarities and differences.

2. Andrew discusses some key ideas in his multicultural-literature teaching. Nearly all of them help children think critically. One of them involves having children examine the poverty markers that represent particular regional or racial and ethnic groups. Review four to six picture books with poverty markers. Note other markers you find interesting, such as those of gender or class. Write a minireview of these books and your findings. To elaborate, add a section to this short paper on how one might use the books to teach critical thinking in a classroom.

3. Examine the latest five to ten Caldecott and Caldecott honor books for multicultural content. Ask yourself, For whom is this book written? Why was it written? To learn more, select a few of the books and read them, asking children for their responses. Compare your responses with those of a colleague or classmate.

John Greenwell: *Teaching and Managing a Multiage Primary Classroom*

Information on John Greenwell's teaching also appears in Chapter 2. In addition to teaching, John's passions include environmental issues, gardening, hiking, camping, and—of course—his dog, Martin. As a former city dweller, John has developed an appreciation for life in a small rural community.

John Greenwell

As you may recall from my introduction to teaching inquiry in a multiage classroom in Chapter 2, I had an interesting conversation with a principal in a job interview. That interview gave me my first job.

Through my conversations with that (wise) principal, it became clear that he liked the philosophy set forth in constructivist-based instruction. I had studied the tenets of social constructivist learning theory and literature-based teaching in my literacy courses, and I knew enough to realize that those things were part of the kind of teaching I wanted to do. As I said in chapter 1 I am very interested in democratic classrooms. However, I had no idea how to create the kind of classroom I wanted. So although my response to the principal (that I could make our philosophy work in sixth grade) was honest, I was also more than a little anxious.

When I got that first job I didn't realize that I was also beginning an extraordinary journey into the world of learning—the children's and my own. After a brief period of teaching sixth grade, I moved to a primary, multiage classroom. In the following section I focus again on this classroom.

It is critical that students have significant input in their school work. This helps ensure authentic learning and independence. Each person is unique, and this uniqueness is maintained by their making choices (Fenstermacher and Soltis 1992). As noted in Chapter 2, it's very important to create a classroom environment in which we all function well. A classroom environment based on my philosophy is a respectful and responsible one in which the teacher and students show mutual respect and have mutual responsibilities. After all, this is what democracy demands of all of us. Accordingly, I sometimes assign explicit topics to help fulfill school curricula or what I deem necessary for children's learning. Every teacher engages in a search for striking such a balance. I have found that seemingly opposing views of independent student learning and explicit instruction work well when carried out well.

In addition to teaching in ways that include all facets of the curriculum, I am very careful that children are not asked to do things that are too challenging for them. Although it is true that children (all of us!) need challenges to continue to learn, it is also true that challenges need to be in the zone of proximal development. For me this means that my teaching points and instructional supports are well scaffolded and at a place at which children can take from them. When children are faced with a task that overwhelms them, they quickly lose interest and often misbehave. Children act out when they feel threatened with something about which they have no confidence.

Differentiated Instruction

In my class of primary, multiage children, I have a wide range of abilities, experiences, and interests. I meet the needs of these students through my view of progressive teaching. The students do not sit in rows and listen to me lecture. Instead, I facilitate, demonstrate, guide, and point out as they work in small groups, individually, and as a whole group. More importantly, I have different expectations for different-aged students. Different expectations lead to differentiated instruction (Tomlinson 1995). This instruction is multifaceted. For example, in addition to holding different expectations for different children, I also assign varying tasks based on what the child needs to know and the instruction that is developmentally appropriate.

Here are some of the strategies I use to enhance student learning across age levels. These strategies are also very applicable in the regular classroom.

- I think about the content that I believe children should know.
- I consider each child, review past performances, look for strengths and weaknesses, and then establish expectations in work at which she or he can be successful.
- I create various groupings (pairs, small groups, and whole class) to provide the experience of success and challenge. Groupings may be based on ability, need, equity, talent, and interest.

In the beginning, this kind of teacher thinking takes time, but I found I became quicker as time went on. With experience I was able to turn mundane lessons into collaborative learning opportunities. These elements contribute to curricular learning and promote good student behavior. As Jones and Jones (1986, 19) note, "Comprehensive classroom management involves using instructional methods that facilitate optimal learning by responding to the academic needs of individual students and the classroom group." This statement tells us we need to attend to every student, something we all know we have to do. This task can seem overwhelming, but with the kinds of teaching I'm recommending it becomes possible—and even routine.

One example of this kind of learning in my classroom took place while we were developing a garden at our school. As we were observing plants and pulling weeds, one student said, "We need a fence around the garden to keep the rabbits out." This was a good idea and one that gave me the opportunity to teach the concept of perimeter. "That's a great idea, but what will we have to do to put up a fence?" I asked. Soon, we developed a project. Through this project, my students used and learned addition, multiplication, and measuring skills, problem-solving strategies, and presentation and communication skills.

Student groupings were established based on specific assignments. They worked in groups measuring various shapes and objects in the room. This was good preparation for new learning or good review to become reacquainted with measurement. Younger students' tasks involved the addition of smaller numbers. Older students were required to convert feet into inches and inches into feet and yards. I posed several problems at different developmental levels and watched the groups of children solve them. I also had two students who "compacted out" of these lessons altogether because they had demonstrated to me their understanding of the concept (Winebrenner 1992). Compacting out means that these students did not take part in this particular lesson because there was no need for them to spend valuable classroom time working on something they already knew. Such students usually work on joint or individual tasks while the majority of the class participates in the assignment.

Our study of perimeter readily moved to the garden itself. In order to maintain a climate of order and learning, I created newer groupings. I combined younger and artistic students in groups to create plans for flowerbeds that would be planted on the outside of the fence perimeter. These students brought in seed and flower catalogues from home and researched annual and perennial plants for their aesthetic and hardiness qualities. Instead of selecting a single best plan, each group had a section of the perimeter to develop and plant. Four of my older students were grouped to handle the more challenging assignment. These students had to measure the perimeter, call hardware stores to price fencing and posts, and then present the plan (we had developed all along) to the school's environmental committee for approval.

The project blossomed, and with school support some funding was granted. Children were engaged in a real-world enterprise within a diverse and supportive cooperative effort. Sixth-grade students were called in to help dig the postholes, and parents took children to purchase the posts and fencing and then aided in the erecting of the fence. The flowerbeds were planted.

All my students learned about perimeter and other math skills, yet they worked at different levels, were engaged, and experienced success. (And *nothing* succeeds like success.) Students were also learning some earth science.

My teaching involves fairly tight planning, which is necessary to keep one step ahead of the class and provide proper direction. But, this is not unusual in any classroom. Once the idea and practice of differentiated instruction is established in the teacher's mind, the implementation becomes routine.

My expectations are high for all students, and I now automatically plan and adjust for levels of development. When planning, I never expect all the children to do the same thing and never at the same time. I've conditioned myself to ask, What would be appropriate for this child? When is the appropriate time for this child to learn this concept?

Once I began to work out my own inquiry-based instruction (see Chapter 2), I found some wonderful ways to enhance student achievement. In addition to improving students' learning about their topic of study and their language arts skills, inquiry-based instruction is consistent with the goals of a democratic classroom. My inquiry-based instruction provides for student voice, practicing decision making, and taking responsibility.

Scaffolded Learning Techniques and Play

Teaching spelling has always been difficult for me, and it was just as frustrating for my students. When I first began teaching, I felt compelled to assign spelling words to the entire class to study and to have a spelling test at the end of the week. This was much the way I was taught and tested.

I struggled with this ritual for about three years in order to please parents and meet the needs of the curriculum. I was slow to realize that, like so many other people, I had a very mistaken view of how spelling is truly taught and learned. I regret to this day the consequences of my teaching in these early years. Students who had difficulty spelling were labeled "dumb," and I was perpetuating the notion that bad spellers won't make it in life. We can all recall getting that one hundred mark on a spelling test and the feelings of superiority it can generate. I found that, more often than not, the same children were prone to gloating about their grades, and this really bothered me. The way I taught perpetuated a system in which some students had to be losers. That old system generated unhealthy responses. I think competition can be good for children, but not this kind! Competition that supports intrinsic motivation and a desire to improve oneself is what I want for my students. I can't believe it took me so long to realize my errors. I tried different methods in order to reach the various levels of students and their abilities. My efforts were in vain.

There were the "here are your twenty words for the week," the "different words for different students," and, of course, the "find ten words and then learn how to spell them" approaches. The only students who succeeded at these exercises were the ones who could already spell well. All I was doing was creating unnecessary frustration in students who had difficulty with spelling but who were talented and bright in other areas. It wasn't until I saw a student teacher conducting a game called Spaceball that it hit me. I have always tried to support children's skill learning and practice through gamelike experiences, so this spelling game really hit home. From birth, children's learning experiences are grounded in play. Games and playful experiences with written language enhance children's intrinsic motivation, which is far preferable to extrinsic motivation. When students are motivated of their own volition, the teacher is relieved from tedious, nonproductive prodding. With this in mind, I adapted (and adopted) the game that I have renamed Spellball.

This game can be utilized for any area of study. For example, it works well in social studies, science, and even math. Using a baseball format, questions about the spelling of a word are asked of the person "at bat." A single hit is a correct response to a simple question, and the degree of difficulty of the question or word raises the hit to a double, triple, or home run. An incorrect answer or spelling is an out, with three outs ending the inning. As a class, we decided that three innings per team would constitute a game.

In Spellball, students are divided into teams of six, with four teams in the class. These teams are equally divided by learning development so that all teams have an even shot at winning. We collect words on an ongoing basis. Words from student-generated studies make up the bulk of the collection, but I insert words and rules that support a student's attention to particular spelling patterns. These words and rules are printed on cards and then labeled. I also use colors to help code the categories of degree of difficulty; for example, red print for singles, blue for doubles, green for triples, and black for home runs. These words are put into one of the many centers that my students attend daily. Students in the spelling and word center can be observed practicing for the next big game. Invariably, my younger students practice the singles, building confidence and then moving on to harder words. The older students find it challenging to hit home runs, therefore expanding their abilities to spell more difficult words. Students work on blends, word families, and word patterns. I intervene when a student needs more support. With Spellball the children compete but without gloating. And individuals are not losers. The children have one another on their teams and are basically kind and understanding of their differences. They also seem to sense that it's the playing of the game and becoming better spellers that matters.

Research shows that spelling tests are not very effective in helping children learn to spell (Rymer and Williams 2000). I believe that the use of Spellball, the spelling and word center, and my minilessons on blends and word families have helped my students become better spellers. This technique has also allowed my students to learn spelling at appropriate levels (Gentry and Gillet 1993) without the pain of failure.

Importantly, the real benefits of utilizing these strategies are evident in the students' writing. I've seen the benefits for emergent writers who have more difficulty expressing their thoughts through writing or those who limit their writing to the words they spell. For the more fluent students, Spellball and my work on improving instruction contribute to learning the rules and exceptions.

What Happens When Students Make Responsible Independent Choices?

Teachers have asked me, "Do your kids ever finish anything? They're always doing so many things at one time!" I find this amusing in that these same teachers are constantly collecting papers, telling the students to hurry up, and then worrying what to do with those who finish early. I've always believed that idle children are potentially children in trouble, both academically and in managing their own behavior. Thus, part of my classroom-management plan is to make sure students are involved in meaningful tasks. First, I make sure that all students have more than one assignment in progress and that we have agreed on deadlines in the initial stages of the project. This allows students to work at a pace that is best for them, and it promotes higher-quality results.

Another classroom feature is that students have independent study time (IST). This is key to inquiry-based instruction and it enables students to extend their projects over time (see Chapter 2). In IST they have twenty or thirty minutes each day to engage in their inquiry project. Each morning, as we review the agenda, students decide on an IST time and sometimes ask for more than one, depending their workload. With a selection of ongoing math, writing, reading, or individual studies, students have choices in their work. I find this time important in that it allows a student to decide what's important or what project might have priority over another due to deadlines, interest, or simply the mood of the student at that moment. At the beginning of each IST, I always have the students ask themselves, "What needs my attention most today?" (Yes, I do this successfully with primary children!)

All students know that I, as the teacher, have the right to ask, "What are you working on?" Thus, IST gives me the opportunity to converse with students one-on-one and to guide and redirect students who might be having difficulties. Many students who have caught up with their work find this an excellent time to do silent reading or play Spellball. We have a postal system in our school, so often IST is a time used to write letters to friends in other classrooms.

IST has saved me hours of headaches in trying to figure out what to do next, especially when children complete projects at different rates. Timing issues are especially common in a multiage classroom or any classroom in which children engage in inquiry projects. All children are unique learners, and using IST acknowledges and respects their differences. But, most importantly, this time provides students with the opportunity to make choices and decisions that, in turn, scaffold self-directed responsibility and independent thinking.

Over the years, I've worked to make the classroom work to create bonds of trust, to help children learn and discover, and to make my job doable and enjoyable. Teachers must find joy in their work.

Once I get to know my students through their writing, our talk, and my observations, I learn their interests. And I can step in and challenge or step back and support. I can decide when to introduce new concepts and to teach democratic principles shown through individual and collective (classroom) rights, responsibilities, and respect. I work to leave no one behind.

As I watch my third-graders, especially those who have been with me for three years, I ask myself if they have learned all that they could have. Likely not, but I know that they have learned a great deal. They have lived in a classroom that honored and supported their thinking and actions and with a teacher who redirected and corrected them when they needed it.

I look at the child who told me she couldn't read when she first came into my classroom. She now reads chapter books with confidence and fluency. I see the impish kid who couldn't spell his name on the first day of school, who now spells words like tremendous and experiment with ease. I recall the first-grader who filled his page with letters that had no meaning to me and now writes legible pages of interesting stories that everyone can read. So, I measure the children's successes and personal growth and consider my own as their teacher. And, as for me, this leg of an incredible trek is only the beginning of something quite wonderful. I love to teach. My students love to learn.

For the Instructional Conversation

In-Class or In-Group Thinking and Action

1. Skim the discussion of John's responses to interviewing for his first teaching job and how he searched for his style during his first year of teaching. (See Chapter 2) Jot down ideas, insights, concerns, and conflicts that connect with your own. Discuss and compare notes in small groups or the whole group. Note common themes.

2. Critical incidents are often stressful events or moments that John sees as essential to his learning to teach. Think of a critical incident in your life in which you learned something under less than pleasant circum-

stances. Connect this to teaching and learning in your classroom. What does this tell the professional educator?

3. Think about the kind of teacher John seems to be and turn to the teacher attributes in Chapter 1. Consider one or more principles that you connect to John's professional development. Discuss why you believe this is true of John and elaborate on your discussion by (a) writing up why you think this principle is important in teaching, or (b) discussing another teacher or mentor you have known who exemplifies this principle.

Reflective Thinking and Action

1. Read a book or some journal articles on multiage classroom teaching. List the positive and negative aspects from your own perspective and that of the author(s). Check for commonalties and differences; write a quick summary and prepare a short discussion about your findings.

2. John quotes Jones and Joncs (1986) on competition. Review this book and another newer book on competition. Write a summary of your findings on competition and particularly on competition in the classroom. Include your personal responses to this issue in the conclusion.

3. Develop a list of inquiry topics for your students, your future students, or the students you have now. Making an outline of possible activities and materials, respond to one of the following two questions.

   (a) How would you incorporate elements of independent thinking, problem solving, and decision making for the students as they engaged in this work?

   (b) How would you organize the student's work for differentiated instruction? Use John's contributions in Chapter 2 and Chapter 5 to support your work.

Chapter Summary

In the personal and professional lives of JoAnn Archie, Andrew Allen, and John Greenwell are similar personal and professional qualities. In all three teachers we see examples of Tharp's principles of effective teaching. One of the most salient examples of his work is in the joint production activity of the teacher and the students. It was in this teaching action that JoAnn, Andrew, and John truly excelled and upon which they built their classroom management and instruction. In addition, these teachers clearly demonstrate that professional development occurs in people who are highly principled and have an abiding compassion for their students.

JoAnn, Andrew, and John held strong beliefs from the very beginning about what they wanted in their own professional lives and in the lives of their students. It takes no small amount of "true grit" to hold onto such beliefs over time. It takes a great deal of hard thinking and learning to put such complex beliefs into action. But, as JoAnn reminds us, "Unless conscious efforts are made to build a sense of community all other teacher know how is futile." *Doing* teaching—that is, putting theoretical, personal, and professional concepts and ideals into everyday classroom action—is the greatest challenge we face. When it happens, we know it just as surely as JoAnn, Andrew, and John do. Key to living a good teaching life is putting aside frustrations and making mistakes work to improve instruction and classroom community. In doing so we better appreciate the children in all their glory.

References

Aardema, V., and M. Brown. 1989. *What's So Funny, Kentu?* New York: Dial Books Young Readers.

Allen, A. 1997. "Creating Space for Discussion About Social Justice and Equity in an Elementary Classroom." *Language Arts* 74 (7): 518–524.

Allen, A. 1996. "'I don't Want to Read This': Student's Responses to Illustrations of Black Characters," In *Educating African Canadians,* ed. K. Brathwaite and C. James, 147–166. Toronto: James Lorimer & Co.

Ayers, W. 1993. *To Teach.* Portsmouth, N.H.: Heinemann.

Bogart, J. 1990. *Daniel's Dog.* Toronto: Scholastic.

Brenner, B. 1993. *Wagon Wheels.* New York: Harper.

Britzman, D. 1991. *Practice Makes Practice.* Albany, N.Y.: State University of New York Press.

Calkins, L. 1990. *Reading Between the Lines.* Portsmouth, N.H.: Heinemann.

Charney, R. 1992. *Teaching Children to Care.* Greenfield, Mass.: NE Foundation for Children.

Cochrane, O., and D. Cochrane, S. Scalena, & E. Buchanan. 1984. *Reading, Writing and Caring.* Winnepeg: Whole Language Consultants.

Coerr, E. 1986. *The Josefina Story Quilt.* New York: HarpTrophy.

Coloroso, B. 1987. *Discipline: Winning at Teaching.* Boulder, Colo.: Kids Are Worth It.

Curtis, B., D. Livingstone, & H. Smaller. 1992. *Stacking the Deck.* Montreal: Our Schools/Ourselves Education Foundation.

Dahl, K. & P. Freppon. 1995. "A Comparison of Inner-city Children's Interpretations of Reading and Writing Instruction in the Early Grades in Skills-based and Whole Language Classrooms." *Reading Research Quarterly.* 30 (1): 50–74.

Dei, G. 1993. "(Re)Conceptualizing 'Dropouts' from Narratives of Black High School Students in Ontario." Presentation paper. Atlanta, Ga.: American Educational Resources.

Delpit, L. 1995. *Other People's Children.* New York: New Press.

———. 1998. "The Silenced Dialogue: Power and Pedagogy in Educating Other People's Children." *Harvard Educational Review* 58 (3): 380–398.

Dudley-Marling, C. 1997. *Living with Uncertainty.* Portsmouth, N.H.: Heinemann.

Edelsky, C. 1994. "Education for Democracy." *Language Arts,* 000–000.

Fenstermacher, G., & J. Soltis. 1992. *Approaches to Teaching.* New York: Teachers College Press.

Fisher, B. 1991. *Joyful Learning.* Portsmouth, N.H.: Heinemann.

Forster, M. 1997. *Black Teachers on Teaching.* New York: New Press.

Freppon, P. 1995. "Low-Income Children's Literacy Interpretations in a Skills-based and Whole Language Classroom." *Journal of Reading Behavior.* 27 (3): 505–533.

Gentry, J., & J. Gillet. 1993. *Teaching Kids to Spell.* Portsmouth, N.H.: Heinemann.

Goodman, K. 1986. *What's Whole in Whole Language?* Toronto: Scholastic Inc.

Goodman, Y. 1978. "Kidwatching: An Alternative to Testing." *Journal of National Elementary School Prinicpals.* 572 (4): 22–27.

Greenfield, E. 1978. *Honey, I Love.* New York: Scholastic.

———. 1988. *Nathanial Talking.* New York: Black Butterfly Children's Books.

Hansen, J. 1987. *When Writers Read.* Portsmouth, N.H.: Heinemann.

Harris, V. 1990. "African American Children's Literature: The First One Hundred Years." *The Journal of Negro Education* 59 (4): 540–555.

James, C. 1990. *Making It.* Oakville, Ontario: Mosaic Press.

———. 1994. "I Don't Want to Talk About It." *Orbit* 25 (2): 26–29.

Jones, L., & V. Jones. 1986. *Comprehensive Classroom Management.* Newton, Mass.: Allyn and Bacon.

Keats, E. 1970. *Hi, Cat!* New York: Aladdin Books.

Kiefer, B. 1983. "The Responses of Children in a Combination First/Second Grade Classroom to Picture Books in a Variety of Artistic Styles." *Journal of Research and Development in Education* 16 (3): 14–20.

Kraus, R. 1971. *Leo the Late Bloomer.* New York: Simon & Schuster.

Ladson-Billings, G. 1994. *The Dreamkeepers: Successful Teachers of African American Children.* San Francisco: Jossey-Bass.

McGinnis, E., & A. Goldstein. 1997. *Skillstreaming the Elementary School Child.* Champaign, Ill.: Research Press.

Mitchell, M. 1997. *Uncle Jed's Barbershop.* New York: Aladdin Paperbacks Simon & Schuster.

Moll, L., & N. González. 1994. "Lessons from Research with Language-Minority Children." *Journal of Reading Behavior* 26 (4): 439.

Mollel, T. 1990. *The Orphan Boy.* Toronto: Oxford University Press.

Moss, T. 1993. *I Want to Be.* New York: Dial Books Young Readers.

Munsch, R. 1993. *Wait and See.* Toronto: Annick Press.

Newman, J. 1984. *The Craft of Children's Writing.* Toronto: Scholastic.

———. 1985. *Whole Language.* Portsmouth, N.H.: Heinemann.

Norton, D. E. 1991. *Through the Eyes of a Child.* New York: Macmillian.

Oldfather, P., & J. West with J. White & J. Wilmarth. 1999. *Learning Through Children's Eyes.* Washington, D.C.: American Psychological Association.

Roop, P., & C. Roop. 1989. *Keep the Lights Burning, Abbie.* Atlanta, Ga.: Houghton Mifflin.

Routman, R. 1991. *Invitations.* Portsmouth, N.H.: Heinemann.

Rylant, C. 1985. *When I was Young in the Mountains.* New York: Dutton.

Rymer, R., & C. Williams. 2000. "'Wasn't that a Spelling Word?': Spelling Instructions and Young Children's Writing." *Language Arts.* 77 (5): 241–249.

Sadu, I. 1993. *Christopher, Please Clean Up Your Room.* Richmond Hill, Ontario: Scholastic.

Shannon, P. 1992. "Overt and Convert Censorship of Children's Books." In *Becoming Political,* ed. P. Shannon, 67–71. Portsmouth, N.H.: Heinemann.

Sims Bishop, R. 1993. "Multicultural Literature for Children." In *Teaching Multicultural Literature in Grades K–8*, ed. V. Harris, 37–53. Norwood, Mass.: Christopher Gordon Publisher Inc.

Smith, F. 1988. *Understanding Reading*. Hillside, N.J.: Lawrence Erlbaum Associates.

Solomon, R. 1992. *Black Resistance in High School*. Albany, N.Y.: State University of New York Press.

Steptoe, J. 1996. *Mufaro's Beautiful Daughters*. Needham Heights, Mass.: Silver.

Strickland, Dorothy, & L. Morrow, eds. 1989. *Emerging Literacy:* Young children learn to read and write. Newark, Del.: International Reading Association.

Tharp, T. G. & R. Gallimore. 1995. *Rousing Minds to Life*. New York: Cambridge University Press.

Tomlinson, C. 1995. *How to Differentiate Instruction in Mixed-ability Classrooms*. Alexandria, Va.: Association for Supervision and Curriculum Development.

Van Galen, J. 1993. "Caring in Community: The Limitations of Compassion in Facilitating Diversity." *The Urban Review* 25 (1): 5–24.

Van Manen, M. 1996. *The Tone of Teaching*. Toronto: Scholastic—TAB Publications.

Wigginton, E. 1986. *Sometimes a Shining Moment* New York: Anchor Books.

Williams, K. 1990. *Galimoto*. New York: Lothrop.

Winebrenner, S. 1992. *Teaching Gifted Kids in the Regular Classroom*. Minneapolis: Free Spirit.

Andrew Allen's Recommended Books

Agassi, M. 2000. *Hands are Not for Hitting*. Minneapolis: Free Spirit.

Barchers, S. 2000. *Multicultural Folktales: Readers Theatre for Elementary Students*. Englewood, Colo.: Teacher Ideas Press.

Barnes, T. 1999. *The Kingfisher Book of Religions*. New York: Laurousse Kingfisher Chambers.

Belloli, A. 1999. *Exploring World Art*. Los Angeles: J. P. Getty Museum.

Bridges, R. 2000. *Through My Eyes*. New York: Scholastic.

Bruchac, J. 2000. *Crazy Horse's Vision*. New York: Lee & Low Books.

Grimes, N. *My Man Blue*. New York: Dial Books Young Readers.

Grossman, M. 2000. *My Secret Camera.* San Diego: Gulliver.

Hopkinson, D. 1999. *A Band of Angels.* New York: Atheneum Books for Young Readers.

Krasno, R. 2000. *Floating Lanterns and Golden Shrines: Celebrating Japanese Festivals.* Berkeley, Calif.: Pacific View Press.

Marx, T. 2000. *One Boy From Kosovo.* Scranton, Penn.: Harper Collins.

Medina, J. 1999. *My Name is Jorge On Both Sides of the River.* Honesdale, PA: Wordsong.

Mitchell, L. 1999. *Different Just Like Me.* Watertown, Mass.: Charlesbridge Publications.

Thimmesh, C. 2000. *Girls Think of Everything.* Boston: Houghton Mifflin.

Whitney, T. 1999. *Kids Like Us.* St. Paul: Redleaf Press.

6

Personal and Professional Development: A Lifelong Process

PENNY FREPPON

In this closing chapter I touch on a few important aspects of this book. The rest I leave to you and to me as we continue to learn about what it takes to be a teacher and the role of personal and professional development in effective teaching.

The teachers in this book show that they learn from literary resources, conversations, and conference experiences. Their practices demonstrate that effective teachers learn from and with the students they teach. The teachers' interior reflective dialogue, their sense of justice, and their view of teaching as a moral endeavor show how the personal and professional become one in learning to teach. In all their professional learning there is personal growth and change, which generates the learning cycle. It takes a lifetime to learn to be fully human and to learn to teach (our human and pedagogical vocation). In the teaching moment we learn and find our humanity.

Just as we adjust to life events with family, friends, colleagues, economics, health, and a myriad of other things, we adjust to our teaching lives. Each new year we learn about new students, new materials, and more. Teachers thrive and renew their energy and themselves in learning and practice.

Attributes and Principles

I began in Chapter 1 with the idea that tension is a valuable experience that often leads the way to personal and professional growth. Teaching tensions are clearly evident in every teacher's classroom life. However, rather than remaining frustrated or becoming defeated by tensions, effective teachers face the mountain before them. They continually work hard on their development as human beings and as professional educators, thereby confirming the axiom that teacher change is key to teaching change. Rather than seeking answers, effective teachers seek to understand the paradoxes of teaching and the mindset of living well in the imperfect world of human learning.

Simultaneous personal and professional development is rooted in the teacher attributes discussed in this book (Ayers 1993). Effective teachers are principled people with a strong sense of responsibility. They enjoy children and have compassion for them. They search for their own strengths and give to themselves ways of using their strengths to be better teachers. Deep within the being of effective teachers is self-respect. For principled teachers, nothing less will ever do for their students.

In similar ways the five principles of effective teaching (Tharp, Estrada, Dalton, and Yamauchi 2001) reveal important elements. Responsible, compassionate, and personally strong people are those fully able to do the following:

- Engage in joint teacher and student productivity.
- Provide contextualized studies that connect to the lives of students.
- Promote language development.
- Create cognitively complex instruction.
- Use instructional conversations that teach complex thinking.

Exemplary scaffolding is shown throughout this book. Such scaffolding is also necessary for teachers' learning and is embedded in the ways teachers learn. Tharp and Gallimore's explication of scaffolding provides a valuable lens through which it may be examined. They hold that joint problem solving and being meaningfully involved, learning by doing, working toward shared goals, attributing competence with warmth and responsiveness, and creating a positive emotional tone are essential. These scaffolds are evident in the instruction shown in this book.

Reflection and Its Importance to Effective Teaching

One of the most salient aspects of the teaching featured in this book is the synergistic and inseparable nature of reflective thinking and action. As noted in Chapter 1, the term *reflection* is echoed throughout teacher education and professional development protects and professional literature. However, the personal and professional experience of reflection is not well understood. Its very nature and structure are unclear.

In their review of the literature on reflection as an object of study, Rosko, Vukelich, and Risko (in press) found that reflection is described by properties of the phenomenon such as teachers' use of it to link theory and action, to move beyond teaching as a field of technical expertise, and to socially construct acts of making decisions and taking responsibility. A complex mix of factors occurring in various professional contexts shapes reflection. Thus, the ability to learn and become more adept at reflection is accessible through a range of professional experiences, such as study groups, action research, professional development work, and university courses.

Deep reflection, however, is far more challenging than one might imagine, because it's one thing to learn to think about aspects of teaching and learning and quite another to develop this thinking into an increasingly effective practice. The concept of reflection as a process of inquiry, or a problem-solution cycle of ongoing thought and action, is essential. The following quotations from some of the teachers in this book help to show some key aspects of reflection.

An excerpt from Donna Ware's journal demonstrates reflection's generative power in helping teachers acquire new ideas.

> Today I read a great book on friendship (in class). We discussed the book and talked about other books on friendship and listed them on the board. Everyone seemed to enjoy it. I gave a suggestion to write a "Friendship Is" book. But it [the enjoyment] didn't last long. I look around the room at my writers and see Conner making a face, Terry staring in to space, Tim staring at the bookcase, and Mitchell, who doesn't have any paper on his desk. Helen Jane, Chris, Tabitha, Michael Aaron, and Jenny are writing, but Tracee is playing with a bottle of mouthwash. Where she got it is a mystery to me—time for me to try another way.

As Donna learned to teach writing, she discovered the ultimate value of children's self-selected topics *and* she learned to provide the explicit support needed for children to succeed in topic selection and use.

This quotation from Phyllis demonstrates the "reframing" that Schone (1987) holds as fundamental. It shows the investigative nature of effective teachers' reflections.

> At one writing workshop conference, Donald Murray taught me one of my most significant lessons about teaching and learning. He asked the participants to free-write, stop, reread our work, and raise our hands if we have written something that we had not originally intended to write. As hands filled the air, he explained that writers, "write to discover what they have to say" (Murray 1967, 9). I was excited about this notion. . . . And it has influenced my teaching ever since. . . . Later I learned to apply this idea to writing about math and science. . . .

When teachers reflect, they do not ignore their beliefs and current knowledge base, but rather . . . "expand on them to take on new perspectives and problematize situations and ideas" (Rosko, Vukelich, and Risko, in press). Knowing that reflection is based on concepts of reframing (seeing ordinary things in a new light) and investigation (studying problematic events) promotes teachers' personal growth and empowers them in practice.

What's Ahead?

If we are to ensure the growth and development of children, teachers' growth and development should also be at center stage. The concept that the best investment in children's learning is in their teachers' learning is of utmost importance.

Beyond teacher education at the university level and the professional development project, the success of teacher learning also depends on the restructuring of the school day and the school itself. Schools no longer house technicians who disperse knowledge to rows of quiet, orderly children. But the majority of schools retain the attitudes and structures of that bygone era. Teachers must have structures and time for growth and development in their place of practice. Teachers belong in graduate education and professional development projects, but they belong all the more in their schools. To be effective, teachers must have opportunities to learn in schools. High-quality, long-term, school-based professional development projects provide an excellent beginning. Then personal and professional development becomes part of the school culture. Once embedded in the everyday life of classroom teachers, clinical study and affirming support on the job will be routine. This will help move classroom practice from the concept of "training" to that of developing the professionals teachers want to be and children so deserve.

Teachers who become effective educators necessarily engage in personal development. They are those who, through struggle and challenges, become satisfied in their work and become the lifelong learners the profession demands. The journeys of the teachers in this book demonstrate this. They also demonstrate that personal and professional development become a self-sustaining and synergistic process in which intrinsic motivation is a central aspect of even the most difficult teaching period.

Although many individual teachers follow the path of personal and professional development shown in this book, it's vital that every teacher make the journey. Our era demands school reform. Improvement is needed, and this is especially true in low-income urban and rural schools. Children of poverty are the major concern. It is this population that is falling behind while middle- and high-income children do well. A vital step toward school improvement, especially for at-risk children, is in making each teacher's learning as important as each child's learning.

The "improvement movement" of today is more than the rational desire for providing better learning opportunities. This movement is part and parcel of a politically driven threat to public education. Charter schools, voucher schemes, and efforts to expand funding to nonpublic schools undermine the public system that sustains and grows the nation in countless ways. Unfortunately, incorrect bad news about test scores and the achievement of public schools abounds, and it has made an impact on the collective consciousness (Berliner and Biddle 1995; Gee 1999. Also see the following web cites for more information.

http://nces.ed.gov/nationsreportcard/reading/read_new_find_avgup.asp
http://nces.ed.gov/nationsreportcard/reading/reading_trends_natl.asp

The good news is that there is a strong research base on which to draw, many dedicated teachers, teacher educators, parents, administrators, and some state and federal legislators and state offices working hard for school reform through teachers' professional growth.

Emphasizing the Personal Aspects of Learning to Teach

Preservice and inservice university courses promote personal growth and development in many ways. Most important are courses that include dialogue on teacher development and classroom community. The rationale and action needed for this kind of dialogue is not sufficiently embedded in typical preservice and inservice experiences. Yet, efforts to improve discourse in the educational community are evident.

Also evident are professional development projects that emphasize the personal. For example, use of Cooperrider and Srivasta's (1990) appreciative inquiry (AI) work provides interesting opportunities. The AI model demonstrates how we can bring possibilities to life and develop our capabilities (Cooperrider and Srivasta 1990; Hammond 1998). The AI model is used in the Ohio CORE professional development project (Rosko 2001). Based on the concept that we get what we focus on, teachers focus on the moments when they felt the most effective and connected in relationships and in the profession. Through an interview process AI taps into "peak" experiences teachers have had in their lives. Interview techniques draw out stories of the best of the past. Interviews set the stage for visualizing what might be. Cooperrider's work promotes:

- Inquiry into "the art of the possible" in teaching life should begin with appreciation.

- Inquiry into what's possible should be applicable and provocative.
- Inquiry into the human potential of a teaching life should be collaborative.

One-on-one interviews increase mutual interest and trust between lead teachers or literacy specialists and other teachers. Teacher-to-teacher interactions generate conversations that contribute to personal and professional development. (See the Appendix for more information and sample interview questions.)

Conclusion

In the preface of this book I wrote that effective teachers are unique in their individual and sociocultural differences. With all their differences, they are people with common goals who enjoy belonging in the profession. When schools become places for teacher learning, the more teachers will learn and the more they will become teacher researchers.

School size, structure of the day, and attitudes cannot be permitted to limit teachers' ability to sit around a table and discuss their feelings and their practice. School culture must provide the milieu in which teachers engage in structured professional discussions throughout their careers. This is accomplished in other cultures admired for educational achievement.

The Japanese believe that teachers need two periods a day to talk about their learning and teach one another (Jim Gee, personal communication, March 2001). This approach is well worth considering on a large-scale basis in U.S. schools. In addition, professional development projects can provide the structure and leadership needed to support teachers in courses or study groups in schools that are more fruitful than most "planning periods." At the heart of it, the idea of teachers sitting around a table and talking about students and their own learning is fundamentally social. Recognition of the necessity of social contexts functioning to support personal and professional growth is key to effective teaching.

To conclude our conversation, the teachers and I think out loud about some of our teaching experiences and how we feel about other teachers featured in this book.

> Reading Donna's journal was an eye-opener for me. How important administrators are. They can make or break a teacher. I've realized through my writing that I learn best through being actively involved with students in the process of their learning. As I've read some of the chapters I am struck by the deep sense of commitment and determination to succeed in spite of some powerful negative forces.

I once spent a week with Carol Avery in a writers' workshop, and she changed me forever as a teacher. With her gentle nudging, she opened doors, some only a sliver, and gave me license to go through with my own writing.

Donna's piece made me think about how I to struggled to cover everything. Not until I gave myself the right to take "baby steps" did I begin to feel the kind of success I wanted. Karen made me stop and think when she wrote, "Children feel safe because tasks were designed with success [built in]. For some children, school is the best place she or he will be in all day, every week, every month, and every year. For that reason alone we have an ethical and moral obligation to work from this understanding.

I use this quotation, "If you are really comfortable with what you are doing, you have probably stopped growing." Teaching is a wonderful way to spend your life; it's never a solo act. It seems we all began with big ideas and a "bag of tricks," rode the waves of success and eddies of failure, and evolved as better teachers as we deepened our theoretical base, became risk-takers ourselves, and eventually empowered our own students.

In reading Karen's piece I am drawn into her description of the tapestry of growth. We are all tapestries, woven by the threads of experience. Effective teachers question the how and why of teaching.

It does us no good to get angry with a child who is not learning or seek reasons outside our control for why the child is not learning. We must not fall into the trap of placing blame on others when it's up to us to teach this child. Ruth uses the words *curiosity* and *in search of*. This reminds me that effective teachers are like pioneers, curious seekers of a better way. In reading various chapters, I'd venture to say that the word *learn* is used more than the word *teach*. We all learn from the children who show us the inadequacies of prescribed curriculum and from the children who sometimes tell us directly what they like or don't like. We learn from many sources, but we always learn from children. We've all experienced our growing pains, but we remain hopeful and have found joy in composing our teaching lives. Our students and we are works in progress.

For the Instructional Conversation and Reflective Thinking and Action

Divide into groups of three to five and have each group choose a different scaffolding premise from the preceding text. Research one teacher of your choice (and her or his comments in Chapter 1). Identify instances from this teacher's personal and professional learning in which your group's scaffolding premise is evident. These instances may be listed and some of them elaborated on by different members of the group. Elaboration may include the member's rationale for choosing a particular event and a deeper discussion of its scaffolding properties.

Engage with one or more of the following topics:

- attributes of effective teachers
- teaching tensions and challenges
- reflection
- ways in which teachers learn, discussed in Chapter 1

As you conclude your discussions, consider ways in which schools might be structured to better support teacher's development of desirable attributes. Are such things innate, somehow preset and fixed, or can the social or cultural world of the school have an influence? Include in your discussion how schools and colleagues could work together on teaching tensions, on respecting teacher's individual strengths, and the kind of reflection that counts in effective teaching. What are the roles and responsibilities of teachers in all this and in their personal and professional development?

References

Ayers, W. 1993. *To Teach.* New York: Teachers College Press.

Berliner, D., & B. Biddle. 1995. *The Manufactured Crisis.* Cambridge, Mass.: Perseus.

Cooperrider, D., & S. Srivasta. 1990. "Positive image, Positive Action." In Appreciative Management and Leadership. San Francisco: Jossey-Bass.

Gee, J. 1999. "Reading and the New Literacy Studies." *Journal of Literacy Research.* 31 (3): 355–374.

Hammond, S. A. 1998. *The Thin Book of Appreciative Inquiry.* Plano, Texas: Thin Book Publishers.

Murray, D. 1967. *A Writer Teaches Writing.* Boston: Houghton Mifflin.

Reading and the New Literacy Studies. 1999. "Reframing the National Academy of Sciences Report on Reading." *Journal of Literacy Research* 31.3 (355–374).

Rosko, K., C. Vukelich, & V. Risko. In press. "Preparing the Reflective Teacher of Reading: A Critical Review of the Professional Education Research." *Journal of Literacy Research.*

Rosko, K. 2001. "Professional development in Early Literacy Instruction: several difficult problems and a messy solution." Paper read at the Colloquium on Early Literacy Instruction for Children At Risk: Research-based Solutions. CIERA. March 24, 2001, University of Michigan, Ann Arbor Mich.

Schone, D. 1987. *Educating the Reflective Practitioner.* San Francisco: Jossey-Bass.

Tharp, R., P. Estrada, S. S. Dalton, & L. A. Yamauchi, 2001 "Teaching Transformed." Boulder, Colo.: Westview Press.

Appendix

Chapter 2
Ruth Heil's Samples

Animal Research Checklist

1. My name is_____

    My animal is_____

2. Write: What I already know about_____

3. What I'd like to learn:

    A. Look at your animal mapping sheet. Think about two categories of information you'd like to study. Talk it over with your group.

    B. Read the questions about that category with your group.

4. Reading Sample: Become acquainted with your animal. Spend time looking through the books, magazines, etc., in your packet. Look at the contents, pictures, and index; read something that interests you.

5. Group Conversation: Share with the people in your group what you learned during your reading sample activity. Do you want to stay with the categories you chose in Step 3?

    Yes_____

    No_____ (If you check no, what are your new categories?)

6. Make sure your group has decided on the two categories you will study. Get your teacher's signature before going to Step 7.

    _____

7. Read through the question paper and *add* any questions to your category that you would like to research.

8. Set up 2 long pieces of paper for your *notes*. One will be for each of your two categories.

Sample:
you'll need
two of
these.

Name _____ Animal _____
Category _____
Questions:
1. _____
2. _____

Animal Research Checklist, page 2

9. Now you are ready to go back to your reading!
   Read to find answers to your questions in each category. You are trying to find these answers so you can talk with the people in your group. Stop every now and then and share what you have learned. *After* you have shared, *write down your notes.* Remember, notes are written in words and phrases, not sentences. Good luck!

10. Make an animal pamphlet with your group. Share the work. Fold your paper in thirds as we did for the animal we did together.

Animal Name Picture	Folder ←cover	Your group's names	*Category* 1. facts 2. 3.	*Category* 1. 2. facts 3.	Inside ←folder	Category (such as food, description, etc.)

11. Write your first draft. Reread your notes, share information with partners, then write by *yourself.* Remember paragraph 1 introduces your animal and your 2 categories of information.

    Paragraph 2   About your 2 categories   ⎱ Remember to include your own
    Paragraph 3   ⎬ experiences, thoughts, and
    Paragraph 4   Closing: 1 or 2 sentences   ⎰ feelings about your animal.

12. Conference with a teacher. Revise if necessary.

13. Brainstorm for a title.

14. Edit. Check for correct information and that it makes sense. Check for capitals, punctuation, and spelling. Did you write your title in capitals?

15. Bibliography: list books in ABC order by author's last name. List only those books, magazines, etc., that you *used* in your research.

16. Put everything in order (directions will be given by the teacher) and put your research in your special writing folder. Turn it in to the teacher.

    You are finished!
    (except for the recopy to do after the teacher does final editing)

Chapter 2
Karen Morrow Durica's Samples

Elkonian Box Teacher and Child Conversation
Reader, as you read this conversation see figures A–1 and A–2.

Teacher: That was a wonderful job retelling that story. What would you like to write about that story?

Child: I want to say, "The crocodile got on."

T: That will be a fun sentence to write. [Here is where teacher can encourage a more complex or a simpler sentence, depending on the needs of the child.] How would you begin the sentence, "The crocodile got on."?

C: With 'the.' I know 'the.'

T: I know you do! Write it on our book writing page. [The book writing page is the page where everything appears correct.]

Child writes the word 'The'.

T: I noticed you put a capital 'T'. Why did you do that?

C: 'Cause it starts the sentence.

T: You are just learning so much about writing! OK, say your sentence again.

C: The crocodile got on. I need crocodile.

T: Yes, let's see if we can work on that one together. What sounds do you hear in 'crocodile'?

C: Is it a 'c' or a 'k'?

T: What do you think?

C: 'c'

T: You got it! What else do you hear?

C: [child stretches word] 'r' and another 'c'

T: There is an 'r' and a 'c'; put the 'r' down and listen as I say the word. What do you hear before that other 'c'? [Teacher stretches word]

C: Oh! I hear an 'ah'. Ah, ah, octopus! 'O'!

T: You are really listening carefully for those sounds. OK, write o and the 'c' you heard. What does that much say?

C: The croc

T: Yes, let's finish this word together [Teacher and student sound word together and collaborate on writing letters—student supplies all but the silent e, which the teacher adds]

So now we have The crocodile; we need to finish the sentence. What did you want to say?

C: The crocodile got on. I need got.

T: I want you to work out got by yourself. I know you can do it! I'll tell you that 'got' has 3 sounds. [Teacher draws 3 lines on the try page; some teachers use boxes]

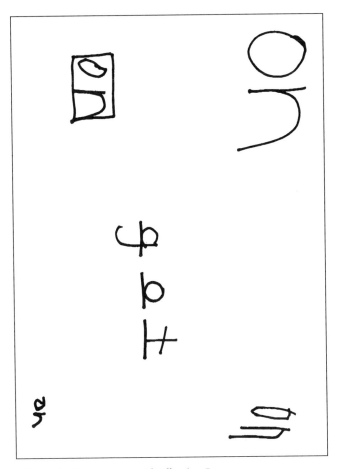

Figure A–1. *Example of Instruction with Elkonian Box*

C: I know it starts with a 'g'

T: Yes, sir! What do you hear next?

C: [Stretches word] A 't'!

T: 'T' is in that word! But where do you hear it. Say it again and listen.

C: 'Got'—it's at the end. 'Got'. oh I know! It's 'o' again! G-o-t

T: Wonderful work! I could just see your brain in action! Now, what do we need to finish your sentence?

C: The crocodile got on. We need on. a-n, right?

T: Let's think about it. You just told me crocodile had an 'o' for the 'ah' sound; and got had an 'o' for the 'ah' sound. So what do you think makes the first sound in ah-ah on?

C: 'o'!

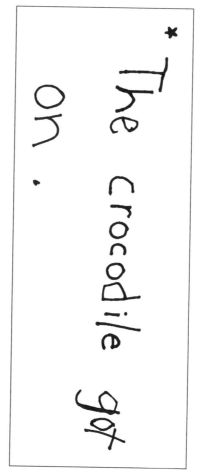

Figure A–2. *Example of Instruction with Elkonian Box*

T: Yes. And you know, on is one of those words it is just good to know right off the top of
   your head. Write 'on' as fast as you can in each corner of the try page. [Child writes
   the word 'on' and says it as it is written.]

T: What's that word?

C: on

T: Draw a box around one of the on's. What's that word?

C: on

T: You are one great writer. Now read the sentence you wrote.

C: The crocodile got on. I like that sentence.

T: Me too!

Differences Between Reading Skills and Reading Strategies

Skills	Strategies
• specific knowledge, ability or proficiency	• plan of action
• unconscious process	• conscious process (metacognitive)
• applied automatically	• applied intentionally
• used inflexibly	• used flexibly and adaptively
• transfer to materials assumed	• transfer to materials must be deliberate
• mastery often expected	• mastery not assumed because level of difficulty influences success

Figure A–3. *Differences Between Reading Skills and Reading Strategies. Adapted from ER & D Reading Comprehension Instruction manual. © 2000 by the American Federation of Teachers.*

Chapter 3
Donna Ware's Samples

WRITING LOG

Name: _____

Poem	Song	Short Story	Essay
Memoir	Letter	Book Review	Other

Date:	Title of Piece:	Genre:	Published:

THINGS I CAN DO DURING WRITING TIME

1. I can add to my topic list.

2. I can brainstorm a new topic.

3. I can begin a new draft.

4. I can revise (improve or add on to) a draft I have started.

5. I can edit my draft:

   look for misspelled words;

   periods and other punctuation;

   words that may need to be capitalized.

6. I can illustrate my draft.

7. I can reread my drafts to decide which one I want to publish or get new ideas to write about.

PUBLISHING JOURNEY

Name: _____ Date: _____

1. Choose a draft you would like to publish.

2. Read your draft to a friend. Use your peer conference booklet.
   I read my draft to: _____

3. Revise. Work on your draft. Add some information or move it
   around. Does your writing grab and hold your reader's attention?

4. Edit your draft by yourself.
   a. Underline any words you think are misspelled. Write them on
      a Have-A-Go.
   b. Look for capitals, periods, or other punctuation. (Use a red
      pen.) _____

5. Put your draft in CONFERENCE BOX 1.
   This is when we share together. I may ask you questions in order to learn
   what you have to teach me. _____

6. Put your draft in CONFERENCE BOX 2.
   During this conference we will look at your editing and discuss one new
   skill you may need to learn to complete your piece. Then you will work on
   your piece.

7. Recopy your piece if you need to. _____
   You only have to recopy your draft if it is too hard to read.

8. Put your draft in the PREPUBLISHING BOX.
   During this conference we will ask you how you want to
   publish your book. You will need to decide if you want a regular book _____,
   a shape book _____, or a big book _____. Will you want illustrations? _____
   Where will the pages start and finish? _____ Do you want an *About the
   Author* page? _____

9. Date book was published: _____

FINDING FOCUS WEB

Choose an idea from your topic list. Write your topic in the center of the web. Brainstorm ideas around your topic.

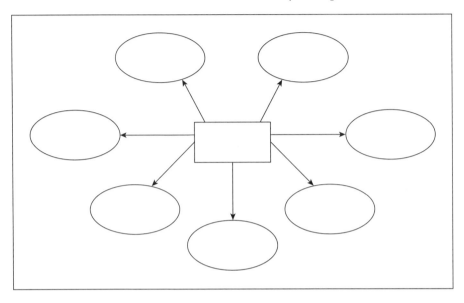

Next, choose one of the events or details you listed around your topic as the center of the web. Brainstorm ideas around your new central idea.

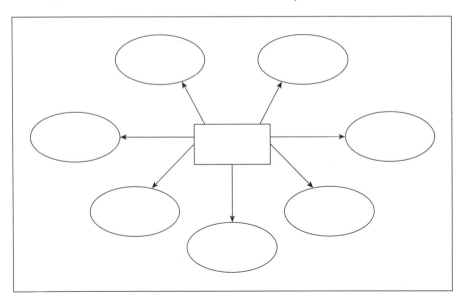

FINDING FOCUS EXAMPLE

Choose an idea from your topic list. Write your topic in the center of the web. Brainstorm ideas around your topic.

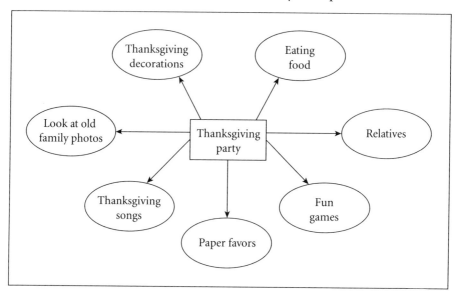

Next, choose one of the events or details you listed around your topic as the center of a new web. Brainstorm ideas around your new central idea.

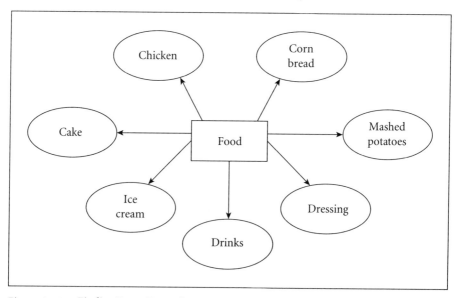

Figure A–4. *Finding Focus Example*

Chapter 4
Phyllis Whitin's Samples

CONSUMER ISSUES STUDY

REQUIREMENTS:

1. Choose an area of interest (many are suggested below). Investigate your interest through research. Some of the methods of research include:
   a. Primary sources
      1. Interview people in business (parents, etc.); write up interview.
      2. Interview consumers (adults, other teens); write up interview.
      3. Study advertisements; keep notes of observations.
      4. Material from Better Business Bureau, Office of Consumer Affairs, Federal Trade Commission, lawyers, etc.
   b. Secondary sources
      1. Read and take notes from books about consumerism.
      2. Read, take notes from magazines such as *Zillions* or *Consumer Report*.
      3. Watch; take notes from videos, filmstrips, or television programs that deal with consumer issues.
      4. Read history of consumer issues; take notes.

YOU MUST USE AT LEAST ONE PRIMARY AND ONE
SECONDARY SOURCE FOR YOUR RESEARCH

2. Sharing your knowledge with others: YOU MUST DO "a" AND "b"
   a. Written component (choose one, DUE 0/0/xx or by arrangement)
      1. Write a letter of action (to FTC, a business, government official).
      2. Create a consumer guide geared to younger audience (pen pals).
      3. Create a consumer guide for same-age audience (team).
      4. Write an informative article about a consumer issue (from history, etc.).
   b. Oral component (2–5 minutes, DUE 0/0/xx)
      1. Talk with visual (enact phone etiquette, give information and explain advertising strategies with a graph, chart, or examples of ads, time line and historical talk).
      2. Share the story of your letter of complaint or letter of action, tell about what you learned, strategies you used to achieve your goal, sources you used.

TOPICS

Marketing analysis	Telemarketing, direct mail, and computer-assisted advertising
Graphic design	What's in the small print—not lying, but . . .

Target groups (i.e. young kids, the health-conscious, teens)
Federal Trade Commission, other agencies (history, actions, etc.)
Ethics (tobacco industry, young children a market)
Issues of stereotypes in advertising (women, the aging, ethnic groups)
Teen's rights in fair service (phone, at the counter, registering complaints)
Tricky words, tricky "statistics" (how to lie with statistics)
Comparative shopping [among stores, catalog vs. retail stores, etc.]

PLEASE COMPLETE THIS PORTION, TEAR OFF, AND RETURN BY 0/0/XX

My topic for my consumer research is: _____

_____	_____
Parent/guardian	Student

Chapter 6
Penny Freppon

Appreciative Inquiry

Appreciative Inquiry is a process that seeks to locate, highlight, and illuminate the best of "what is" in teachers' lives as a point of departure for "what might be." The intent is to sharpen professional vision around successes of a person and the system and then to make these successes more constant in the future endeavors. As a result, teacher *and* school join together to coconstruct a more ideal future that creates large amounts of energy (intellectual and social bonding) needed for lasting change (Rosko 2001).

AI is realized in an interview technique that uses well-thought-through questions for eliciting stories upon which participants may draw for future growth. Questions are focused on topics as indicated in the sample questions. For more information on AI, see Cooperrider and Srivasta (1990) in the references in Chapter 6 and these web sites: www.hskids-tmsc.org, www.hskids-tmsc.org/infocenter/huides/ai_intro.htm.

Sample Interview Questions

1. Thinking back over your years as a classroom teacher (administrator), can you think of a time when you felt deeply energized and excited—a time when you acted with authenticity and where you contributed to the magical unfolding of authenticity in another?

2. Can you think of a time in your teaching (or learning) career when you felt that someone really listened to you and truly heard what you were saying? Who listened? How did you know that you had her or his undivided attention? What was it about this particular person that made you feel that you had truly been heard?

3. Can you tell me about another time when you extended deep listening to another? What was the impact on the other person? What was it about you, your unique qualities as a person, that contributed to the experience?

4. Think of a time when another person helped you reach your potential through their ability to acknowledge, accept, and appreciate the essence of who you are. Tell me that story. What was special about this person, your relationship, or this particular encounter? How did you know that this individual truly understood and accepted the "real" you? How did this make you feel? What happened as a result of the deep knowing? (Prompts: Tell me the story and about contributions of your unique personal qualities. What about other(s), context, leadership, or relationships that contributed to the wonderment of this particular experience?)

Index